intentional
walk

more devotions
for baseball fans

HUGH POLAND

JUDSON PRESS
PUBLISHERS SINCE 1824
VALLEY FORGE, PA

Intentional Walk: More Devotions for Baseball Fans

Library of Congress Cataloging-in-Publication Data
Poland, Hugh.
Intentional walk : more devotions for baseball fans / Hugh Poland.
p. cm.
Includes bibliographical references and indexes.
ISBN 978-0-8170-1543-5 (pbk. : alk. paper) 1. Christian life. 2. Baseball fans—Religious life. 3. Baseball—Religious life—Christianity. I. Title.
BV4501.3.P64 2009
242'.68—dc22   2008042663

Printed on recycled paper in the U.S.A.
First Edition, 2009.

CONTENTS

For mom, who still plays

foreword

An inherent busyness seems to be hopelessly attached to life. You hit the ground running and never look back. Sometime between hitting the snooze button for the last time and before you actually sit up, perhaps you voice a simple prayer. While the prayer may be more out of duty than passion, you may have a few moments when you experience a surge of God's power, like Peter did in Matthew 14 when he stepped out on the water. Then your feet hit the floor, you take a few steps, and you begin to sink like a stone in the craziness of the everyday.

Suddenly you're in a panic and just as you're about to go under, you take notice of the only One who can save you. You cry out and immediately a hand reaches out to grab you.

You are saved. Not by the wind or the waves. Not by anyone in the boat behind you. No, you are rescued by the outstretched hand of Jesus Christ. You end up in the place you should have been to begin with—in his grasp.

It's easy to wonder how Peter could have been so weak in his faith. After all, he had the Son of God bidding him to come, telling him it was safe to take that first step onto the sea. Even though one step onto the water may have been sufficient for you and me to feel God's power, Jesus allowed more than that. Matthew says Peter *walked*, which by definition means he took more than one step. The issue wasn't the lack of power available to Peter; it was the lack of Peter's own focus, his own intent. If Peter had taken an intentional walk that day, his eyes would have never left the King of kings and he wouldn't have found his knees at fish level.

We would do well to start out every single day with an intentional walk for that is what pleases God. To have our attention and efforts focused on one thing; God's power is what helps us walk on top of the water and gives us a hand to grab when we falter. We will always be aware of the waves around us and the water below, but we must never take our eyes off the Savior who forever stands before us.

I have met such an intentional man and am even privileged to call him friend. Hugh Poland is one who pursues his walk, his ministry, and his life in an intensely intentional way. If that intent were to bring attention and honor to himself rather than to God, I would tell you to deposit this book into the nearest receptacle and run for your life. But Hugh is a man of compassion, conviction, and integrity, so I encourage you to take an intentional walk through every last one of these pages.

Baseball fans will be encouraged, entertained, and motivated with stories of some of the all-time greats of the game. And if that weren't enough, Hugh uses his passion for the game and his commitment to the Lord to weave each story into a devotion that will challenge you to a deeper more passionate relationship with Christ.

The truths contained in this book will give you the feel of having the ball in your glove, the bat in your hands, and the dirt beneath your spikes. More importantly though is that you will be left wanting to score the winning run. It's time to play ball, and the manager has just signaled for an intentional walk. "Ball four!"…take your base.

—Kent Bottenfield
Christian recording artist and
former Major League Baseball pitcher

introduction

"Dear friends, this is now my second letter to you. I have written both of them as reminders to stimulate you to wholesome thinking," wrote Peter (2 Peter 3:1). And though Peter never played baseball, he surely was an all-star on the early teams of apostles, leaving us a host of stories and statistics about his life and ministry.

This little book that you hold in your hands is a sequel to *Steal Away: Devotions for Baseball Fans*. If you're an ardent fan or student of the game, you probably won't read any statistics or stories here that you haven't heard before. Bill James or Larry Ritter I'm not.

But in this "second letter" my desire is to help the reader see even more parables in this great game, stories that can inspire us to read God's Word and incorporate it into our lives. "You see, you spend a good piece of your life gripping a baseball, and in the end it turns out that it was the other way around all the time," wrote Jim Bouton in his memorable book *Ball Four*. It's my hope that as you grip God's Word, it will gain an even stronger grip on your life.

Everybody has a baseball story, whether it's of a time they played or when they sat in the stands watching someone else play. After *Steal Away* came out, many people wrote to me and asked if I was related to Hugh Poland, a major league catcher during the 1940s. I am not, but I am related to other Hugh Polands—my father and my late grandfather. Others have asked if I ever played ball myself, and the answer is that although I was legendary in my own backyard, when it came time for public competition, I quickly discovered that my gifts lay in other areas. In fact, you might say that I inherited some of my ball-playing ability from my grandfather Hugh Poland.

"Popo" Poland, as I knew him, had been a catcher on sandlot and company-sponsored teams as a young man. During one game some-time during the 1910s, he was receiving behind the plate when he heard a noise that was very strange to him, a sound in the sky unlike anything that he had ever heard before. He rose from his crouch and took his mask off, and for the very first time in his life, he saw an airplane, fly-ing in the distance. He stood there, slack-jawed, staring at the miracle and beauty of flight, a simple farm boy who couldn't have been less aware of how new technology would radically shape his future in the coming decades.

His impatient pitcher, however, was more concerned about the game at hand and didn't share my grandfather's appreciation for that which had "slipped the surly bonds of earth."[1] Eager to resume play, he threw a fastball toward the plate. It caught my unsuspecting grandfather on the chin and knocked him out cold. This probably explains why he wanted to duck every time he saw an airplane in the sky from that point on. It also explains why "Keep your eye on the ball" is an adage that we Polands take very seriously.

I should mention that the recording company of my friend Kent Bottenfield is the inspiration for the title of this book. When I first met this former all-star pitcher turned contemporary Christian music artist, I asked him what the name of his company, IBB Records, meant. He connected the dots for me as he explained that "IBB" is simply a way of indicating on a scorecard an intentional walk. "BB" designates a base on balls, and the "I" in front indicates that it was intentional.

I want an intentional walk with Christ. I want it to be purposeful, not by accident. Sure, I'll never be able to play ball on the same field with the players mentioned in this book (though maybe someday in another time and another place?). But I get to first base with God the same way they do: by God's grace. And I want to live in that grace on purpose—every day.

I am inspired by and indebted to the Society for American Baseball Research (SABR), particularly the research efforts of Steve Steinberg and Cort Vitty. My special baseball buddies at Woodridge—Dale, Bob, Rod, and Hank—also encourage me with their friendship. I also want to thank those who granted me interviews, including current and former players, such as Morgan Ensberg, Tom Griffin, Bobby Doerr, Al Worthington, Don Kessinger, and Willie Mays Aikens.

As always, the good folks at Judson Press know how to encourage a writer. There were times when I thought that I wouldn't be able to finish this project, but Rebecca Irwin-Diehl and Kim Shimer are full of ideas on how to pitch each story and Scripture combination. They are a battery that any writer would want on the roster.

Finally, "Team Poland" serves as my inspiration every day. My wife, Karen, and daughters, Kayse, Jayme, and Ally, constantly teach me about life and the lordship of Christ. I can hardly believe that God lets me be a part of their lives every day.

Keep your eye on the ball—and the prize (Philippians 3:14)!

first

COSTELLO: "Who's on first?"
ABBOTT: "That's right."
—Bud Abbott and Lou Costello, *Who's on First?*

And watch'd him how he singled…
—Richard, in *The Third Part of King Henry VI*, by William Shakespeare

First basemen who tie themselves in knots are not popular
with second basemen, third basemen and shortstops.
—Whitey Lockman, 1952 all-star first baseman

For what I received I passed on to you as of first importance: that
Christ died for our sins according to the Scriptures, that he was buried,
that he was raised on the third day according to the Scriptures.
—1 Corinthians 15:3-4

the little things

So he said to me, "This is the word of the
LORD to Zerubbabel: 'Not by might nor by power,
but by my Spirit,' says the LORD Almighty....
"Who despises the day of small things?"
—Zechariah 4:6, 10

Baseball is a game of inches.
—Branch Rickey

Do enough 15-cent things right in baseball and you may win.
Let those smallest parts slide and try to rely on
$100 achievements—spectacular events—and you will lose.
—Ray Kroc, owner of the San Diego Padres

A baseball game isn't usually won or lost because of one swing of the bat or one pitch. Actually, it's a series of things done or not done that makes the difference. Hitting the cut-off man. Hustling on every play. Knowing beforehand what you will do with the ball if it's hit to you. Positioning yourself in the right place in the field. Knowing when to take a pitch. Being aware of the strength of the right fielder's arm when you are on base. Coaches often tell players that the little things a player does will make or break the game. No one took this to heart more than the player with the highest lifetime batting average, Ty Cobb.

Cobb, who spent his glory years with the Detroit Tigers, was among the most feared and hated players of all time. He would sharpen his spikes to inflict pain on anyone who stood between him and a base. He rarely had a kind word to say about anyone. He fought and scrapped his way to excel at the game, retiring with 4,189 hits and the Mount Everest of batting averages, .366.

Cobb's all-time record for hits wasn't surpassed until Pete Rose did it in the 1980s. And up until the 1970s, Cobb held the all-time record for stolen bases, with 892. Since that time, his record has been surpassed by Lou Brock and Rickey Henderson. But for almost fifty years Cobb held the record.

Ty wasn't a home run hitter in the pattern of Babe Ruth, but rather a slashing singles hitter who had blinding speed and could leg out many an infield hit. And once he reached first base, he invariably began to kick the bag over and over while the pitcher worked the next batter.

Once a reporter asked Cobb about his nervous habit of kicking the bag. "I was definitely not nervous when I was on first base," Cobb said in his Georgian drawl. "But very early in my career, I discovered that if I kicked the first base enough times, I could move it a full two inches toward second base, which gave me that much of a jump toward stealing the base."[1]

Two inches doesn't sound like much at all. But then again, how many plays at second base seem to be a matter of inches? And Cobb was indeed the all-time stolen base leader for almost fifty years. We wouldn't advocate cheating in the game, but it is remarkable that Cobb consistently looked for even the tiniest advantage over his opponent.

It's the little things we do that are future investments in our character too. Character is made or unmade not by one big decision, but rather by a series of small decisions. How we will react when offended. What we will set before our eyes. Who our companions will be. What we will do when we see someone in need. Where we will choose to get our help.

Valuing truth above convenience. Choosing to seek and worship the Lord even when we don't feel like it.

You have an opponent (Satan) who is out to defeat you. Look for any small advantage that you can find over your sworn enemy, and then exploit it to the fullest. Who are you when no one is looking? Are you doing the little things that will make you a winner in the game of life? God may not have called you to success, but God certainly has called you to be faithful and obedient. The apostle Paul wouldn't have understood the need to swing to protect a runner, but he did understand the need to excel in the little things. "Let us not become weary in doing good," he wrote in Galatians 6:9, "for at the proper time we will reap a harvest if we do not give up."

intentional walk: This week, memorize Psalm 119:11: "I have hidden your word in my heart that I might not sin against you." Quote it to yourself at least five times a day for a week. It may be exactly the little seed of motivation that you need to begin allowing Scripture to become a big part of your life.

there *is* crying in baseball

Record my lament;
list my tears on your scroll—
are they not in your record?
Then my enemies will turn back
when I call for help.
By this I will know that God is for me.
—Psalm 56:8-9

It's not the honor you take with you,
but the heritage you leave behind.
—Branch Rickey, Dodgers general manager who signed Jackie Robinson

As a player, Branch Rickey had a very forgettable major league career. In fact, he probably wished that more people would forget about the one major league record he set that still stands today: as a no-hit, no-field catcher with the New York Highlanders in 1907 (they became the Yankees in 1913), he once allowed thirteen stolen bases in a single game.

But as a general manager in the front office, Rickey changed the face of the game in many ways. He was the first to develop the minor league clubs as a "farm system" for his major league club (at the time, the Cardinals). He developed the first full-time spring training facility (for the Dodgers) and was instrumental in making everyday use of things such as batting helmets and pitching machines. He helped found and fund the Fellowship of Christian Athletes in the 1950s. He put together the components of three different teams that went on to win the World Series (Cardinals, Dodgers, and Pirates). And then, of course, he changed the face of baseball forever when he signed Jackie Robinson to a contract.

Some have suggested that Rickey was simply trying to find a way to attract even more fans to Dodger games, that his breaking of the so-called gentlemen's agreement to ban African Americans from major league baseball was simply a financial issue and not a noble cause. But Rickey was a man of outspoken faith, guided by his Christian upbringing and Methodist roots. His heart had been deeply moved by an episode in his life when he was a much younger man, coaching the Ohio Wesleyan University baseball team.

The team had taken a road trip to play Notre Dame in South Bend, Indiana. When they arrived to check into their rooms, the hotel manager said to Rickey, "I have rooms for all of you—except for him," pointing to the team's black catcher, Charley Thomas.

"Why don't you have a room for him?" Rickey asked.

"Because our policy is whites only," said the hotel manager.

After much discussion between the adamant innkeeper and the persistent Rickey, it was agreed that Charley Thomas could stay in Rickey's room on a cot. After assigning the other players to their rooms, Rickey went up to his room to find Thomas sitting in a chair, weeping and pulling at the skin on his hands, crying out, "It's my skin. If I could just tear it off, I'd be like everybody else. It's my skin; it's my skin, Mr. Rickey!"

That moment seared its way into Rickey's conscience. He was so moved by the young man's despondency and the injustice of his plight that he later said, "For 41 years I have heard that young man crying. Now, I am going to do something about it."[1] And he did. American historians often mark the day that Robinson signed a contract with Rickey and the Dodgers as a major date that helped galvanize the coming civil rights movement.

God hears our cries, too, and does something about it. Our tears move God. In fact, Psalm 56 indicates that God writes it down when we cry. God has compassion on us, longs for justice for us, and remembers our plight.

Another translation of the Hebrew word behind "scroll" in Psalm 56:8 is "wineskin," or in our vernacular, "bottle." If you were to go inside a Middle Eastern tomb from biblical times, you would probably see collections of bottles that were used to collect the tears of mourners at funerals. These vials were then entombed with the loved one as symbols of honor and affection.

Someday, in heaven, God will wipe every tear from our eyes (Revelation 21:4), but until then, it's a great comfort to know that God doesn't view our pain and sorrow with indifference. Jesus himself wept (John 11:35), so he knows grief and sorrow up close. God is the heavenly statistician who records the tears that fall from your eyes and stores them in bottles. God misses no point of pain, forgets no moment of loneliness or depression, and records every teardrop caused by happiness or joy. When injustice has happened to you, you can be assured that God knows, cares, and is for you.

Those hands that attempted in vain to peel off skin of a different color later became the hands of a highly skilled dentist. Just as Branch Rickey remembered that young man's great sorrow, Dr. Charles Thomas never forgot what Branch Rickey did for him. Years later, at Rickey's funeral, the officiating minister said, "Branch Rickey has been called the master mind of baseball. His vision made him that. But, he was also the master heart of baseball....He made goodness attractive to others."[2] Isn't that true of all heroes? Wouldn't it be great if people could say that about you?

intentional walk: God, sometimes I hold back my tears, thinking that it's undignified or a sign of weakness to cry. But I remember today that Jesus cried, and he possessed more dignity and strength of character than any other human being. I know that you are for me, and that my prayers are marked "Special Delivery" when they arrive, bathed in tears, at your throne room. And as I cry out to you, remind me, "Those who sow in tears will reap with songs of joy" (Psalm 126:5).

your ticket is punched

We have peace with God through our Lord Jesus Christ,
through whom we have obtained access by faith into
this grace in which we now stand. And we rejoice
in the hope of the glory of God.
—Romans 5:1-2

I have never once felt threatened or uncomfortable in the
shadows of Yankee Stadium. It is a fortress, not only for those
who come to it, but for baseball itself as well. Inside, the game is
safe from change, preserved as it was 70 years and several
generations ago. The House That Ruth Built, DiMaggio Graced,
Mantle Lifted and Reggie Rocked feels like home to me.
—Steve Wulf, sportswriter, *Sports Illustrated*, August 2, 1993

For eighty-five years the corner of East 161st Street and River Avenue in New York has been the center of the baseball universe, at least according to Yankee fans. "The House that Ruth Built" has seen the greatest players that the game has ever had to offer grace its field, so great that a last name or a nickname is enough to immediately identify them: Ruth, Gehrig, DiMaggio, Ford, Mantle, Berra, Jackson, Jeter, A-Rod, Rivera—and many, many, many more.

The team has won twenty-six World Series titles in its history, which averages out to about one championship every three and a half years. No other baseball team is even close. "Rooting for the Yankees is like rooting for U.S. Steel," says the old axiom, and it's why you either love or hate the Yankees.

In 2008 my good friend Wally blessed me with the chance to go see the Yankees play in Yankee Stadium before it was torn down to make way for the new Yankee Stadium to open in 2009. And when I say "blessed me," it's because he paid for the plane fare, the hotel costs, and game tickets. He grew up in New York, and once a Yankee, always a Yankee. He was trying, in a not-so-subtle way, to sell me on the timeless look of pinstripes.

We took a plane to New Jersey, a train to New York, and a subway to the Bronx, arriving in time to watch batting practice and tour Monument Park. Lining up to walk beyond the center field fence and see the granite and bronze that served to honor past Yankee stars was a thrill for me. Despite the fact that fans were shoulder to shoulder, there was a hush over the place, as if we were in a stately cathedral or a cemetery (comedian Billy Crystal once confessed that as a boy, he thought that Babe Ruth was buried under the big granite slab that bore his likeness).

The game, played in a cold rain, was anticlimactic compared to the rich experience of simply being there. And in between hot dogs, I tried to imagine all the history that the stadium had seen. Joe DiMaggio gliding in center field. Lou Gehrig at a microphone near home plate, declaring himself to be the luckiest man on the face of the earth. Miller Huggins, Joe McCarthy, Casey Stengel, Billy Martin, and Joe Torre pacing in the dugout, trying in vain to keep the clubhouse from exploding between championship seasons. Babe Ruth running the bases in a home run trot, unable to see his spindly ankles and feet because of his big stomach. Yogi Berra jumping into Don Larsen's arms after Larsen pitched a perfect game in the 1956 World Series.

And numbers serve to hallow the experience as well, as if there are some numbers in Yankee history that even non-Yankee fans know and understand: 714, 1927, 61, 26.[1] So much history. In that place, I could not help but feel that I was in the presence of greatness, as if the legendary "mighty men of David" lurked around the corner, or the twelve apostles were watching. If New York is the heaven of the baseball universe, then Yankee

Stadium, particularly Monument Park, is its throne room.

And the only way I got there was that a friend bought my ticket, which guaranteed me access to see it all. There's no way that they would have let me through the gates of the stadium without a ticket. But as great as the experience was, it pales compared to entering the gates of God's presence with thanksgiving and entering God's courts with praise (Psalm 100:4).

When it comes to accessing the throne room of God, your admittance to the courts of heaven is not based on anything that you've done; it's what Jesus did for you at the cross. Jesus is your "ticket." He gives you the right to stand before God the Father and rejoice, not recoil in fear. Yet too often people shrink back from approaching God in personal or corporate worship because they feel unworthy.

Have you ever tried to worship on Sunday morning after you've blown it on Saturday night? You stand to join in the praise, but your face flushes with resentment and shame as you turn your eyes away from people around you. "Nope, better not sing today," you say to yourself as you cross your arms. "I'm just not worthy."

Well, you're right. You're not worthy. But neither are your friends and family or, for that matter, any of the people in the pews around you, or even the worship leaders on stage. None of us are worthy, on our own, to approach God about anything. But the best worship is done by faith, from a heart that knows that it's unworthy and yet continues to declare the worth of God.

By the way, that's the definition of the word *worship*—to declare the worth of God. To acknowledge that the value of knowing God is greater than any other treasure that you could ever pursue.

And that's the beauty of grace. It meets you where you are, the way you are. Grace doesn't require you to clean yourself up before you worship God. Grace cleanses you *as* you worship God. It's a special pass that grants you access to the locker room of heaven, not to dwell on the memories of mortals of the past, but rather to gaze upon the presence of the one true, living God.

Jesus gives you access to the heavenly Father. He gives you the ticket and punches it, and then you get to humbly yet boldly walk into the presence of God as if you belong there—because you do.

intentional walk: I want to worship you wholeheartedly, Lord Jesus, but there are times when I ignore you or run from you, usually because there is sin in my life that I don't want to face up to. Please forgive me for staying away so long, for thinking that I have to clean myself up before I can assemble with your people and worship you. Thank you for grace that allows me to stand in your presence, clean and unafraid.

babe on babe

Am I now trying to win the approval of men, or of God?
Or am I trying to please men? If I were still trying to please men,
I would not be a servant of Christ.

—Galatians 1:10

Whenever an umpire settles down to reminisce about his career,
he will invariably begin with the six most accurate words in the
English language: It wasn't funny at the time.

—Ron Luciano, major league umpire and author

The nickname "Babe" was applied to many players a hundred years
ago. It referred not only to a person's youth, but also to a person's lack
of experience, like calling someone "green" or "wet behind the ears."

Babe Ruth was certainly the most famous. But on one summer afternoon early in the 1935 season, Babe met another Babe, and one taught the other a valuable lesson.

This kind of statement causes small wars among baseball fans, but here goes: Babe Ruth probably is the greatest player in the history of the game. There are the 714 home runs, the lifetime .342 batting average, the way he changed the game from a contest of speed and sacrifice to a "swing for the fences" bombardment. But before he became an everyday outfielder, he was a pitcher who sported a lifetime 94–46 record with a 2.28 ERA. His record of 29 2/3 consecutive shutout innings in the World Series stood for more than forty years. Even today his name is synonymous with being the best. Top performers in any sport or discipline are often referred to as "The Babe Ruth of…."

But all careers must eventually wind down. Toward the end of his career, an overweight and out-of-shape Ruth was sold to the Boston Braves in order to boost ticket sales for the struggling franchise. He played only the first two months of the season for the Braves, and then he retired. It was while playing for the Braves that the veteran Babe met the rookie Babe.

Ralph Arthur "Babe" Pinelli had a respectable albeit short career as a third baseman in the 1920s, during which he only hit five home runs.

After he retired in 1927, he missed the game, so he started all over and trained to become an umpire. He made his debut in 1935, and one afternoon he was working behind the plate when Ruth came to bat.

Ruth stepped into the box, and the pitch was on the corner of the plate. Pinelli raised his right hand and called, "Strike one!" Ruth turned and yelled at Pinelli. "There's forty thousand people in this park that know that was a ball, tomato-head!" Pinelli didn't respond in anger. "Perhaps," he said thoughtfully, "but mine is the only opinion that counts."[1]

The men in blue are accustomed to the boos and taunts of the fans. But the integrity of baseball is dependent upon these men. They must make the calls to the best of their abilities, with no bias, and tell the truth, even when the crowds around them disagree with the call.

Sometimes we try to live our life following Ruth's appeal to the crowd, appealing to the popular opinions of our culture, being more concerned about what the masses say instead of what God says about our lives. "Hey, God! That's not fair! You missed that last call! Everyone down here knows how life should really be!" We might not say those words out loud, but the intention is there.

But truth doesn't bend. You can accept it or deny it, but it's still the truth. Ultimately, God doesn't have opinions. God is right in all things.

If God chooses to respond to us in our anger, I suspect that our Creator, might say wryly, "Mine is still the only opinion that counts."

Babe Pinelli went on to have a fine second career as an arbiter. He was behind home plate for Jackie Robinson's first game, and his last game calling balls and strikes was Don Larsen's perfect game in the 1956 World Series. It is said that after the Larsen game, Pinelli went into the umpire's locker room and cried. Interestingly enough, Pinelli's answer to Ruth probably was formed by his own understanding of God's place in his life. "I have found peace and help in humble, daily prayer when I praise God for His goodness and ask Him to forgive me my trespasses, as I forgive others, and beg His blessings for myself, and my family and friends," wrote Pinelli. "My God...has given me a personal destiny and ...deserves all praise and service."[2]

intentional walk: Lord, help me to listen to your voice as the source for truth in my life. May I never be swayed by the sheer number of others around me, but may I carefully weigh the truth as revealed in your Word and always find it to be sufficient for how to live my life. Help me to live daily for the praise of only one—you.

the fading glory of kings

As a father has compassion on his children,
so the LORD has compassion
on those who fear him;
for he knows how we are formed,
he remembers that we are dust.
—Psalm 103:13-14

It's a mere moment
in a man's life between an
All-Star Game and an old-timers game.
—Vin Scully, longtime Dodgers broadcaster

Baseball is a funny, fickle game that mirrors life in many ways. One minute you're on top of the world, having great success. If you're a pitcher, your fastball looks like the size of an aspirin to the hitters.

If you're a hitter, the ball looks the size of a beach ball when the pitcher throws it. The fans shout your name and want your autograph when you come back to the dugout. If only it would be this way every day, right? Of course, we know that's not the nature of the game. Even the best hitters get it right only three out of ten times. And fame is fleeting. Just ask Mike Kelly.

What? You've never heard of Mike Kelly, the king of baseball? You can't be serious! He was only the best baseball player of his time.

Ever execute a hit-and-run on the field? King Kelly made it popular. Ever steal a base and end with a hook slide? Kelly came up with that sliding strategy. And why does your catcher often run down the line to back up first base? Because King Kelly did it first. Do your pitcher and catcher use signs to communicate? Yes, it was Kelly who thought that up too. He was regularly among the league leaders in runs scored, stolen bases, and batting average. In fact, he once stole six bases in a single game. Playing for Chicago in the '80s, he and the team won five championships.

His name still doesn't ring a bell? Oh, did I neglect to mention that it was the *1880s*?

Kelly was such a great base stealer that a song was written about him entitled "Slide, Kelly, Slide!" The song, recorded on cylinder, was the first pop song of its kind recorded in America, and it was recorded at the studios of Thomas Edison himself. The song wasn't just number one on the charts; it was the *only* thing on the charts.

He was the first baseball player to write an autobiography. So was his face, as portraits of him sprung up in taverns and saloons in Chicago and Boston. He is considered one of the first celebrities to popularize autographing. Kelly carried himself with style and pizzazz, and he was a star on the vaudeville stage. He was so popular that a movie was made later about his life, and he was voted into the Baseball Hall of Fame in 1945.

And then, just as suddenly as his star had risen, it fell. Kelly tragically died of pneumonia at the age of thirty-six. His final words were reported to be "This is my last slide."

Pop artist Andy Warhol once said, "Everyone will be famous for 15 minutes."[1] But it doesn't last. You may find some fame for a little while, but it's like a flower that blooms in the morning and by sunset has withered. And it's the arrogance of every generation to think it won't happen to them. "I won't get old. I'm ten feet tall and bulletproof. I'm going to be young forever." I can imagine that's what Mike Kelly thought. And he certainly had it all. But who has even heard of him today?

You and I and King Kelly have something in common. One hundred years after our life is finished, few will remember or care. But God will know. From everlasting to everlasting, God will know, and God will remember in love all that we did in his name. If life really is here today and gone tomorrow, then we'd better be deliberate about living. We'd better have an intentional walk with Christ.

intentional walk: Lord, please forgive me for chasing my little dreams and schemes and trying to find life apart from you. I don't want to pursue fame for the sake of being famous. I don't want to pursue riches for the sake of being wealthy. Instead, help me to pursue a life with you, and if there are any who recognize my name one hundred years from now, may it serve to inspire them toward their own walk with you.

death of a dream

I tell you the truth, unless a kernel of wheat falls to the ground and dies, it remains only a single seed. But if it dies, it produces many seeds. The man who loves his life will lose it, while the man who hates his life in this world will keep it for eternal life.

—John 12:24-25

When I first signed with the Yankees, the regulars wouldn't talk to you until you were with the team three or four years. Nowadays the rookies get $100,000 to sign and they don't talk to the regulars.

—Lefty Gomez, Hall of Fame pitcher

When you say "The Rookie," baseball fans know that you're not just talking about any first-year player, but the story of "The Rookie," Jim

Morris. The fact that he didn't post Hall of Fame numbers while pitching in the big leagues is not the issue. The fact that he even made the big leagues is the real story.

Morris was a star athlete in high school, and his dream was to pitch in the big leagues. He was drafted in 1982, and he knocked around in the minor leagues for a few years getting to know the surgeons of different ball clubs on a first-name basis. Due to injuries and a lack of maturity, he consistently underachieved on the mound. By the age of twenty-four, he had given up on his dream and his oft-repaired left arm, and he returned to school to get his degree and become a high school science teacher and baseball coach in Big Lake, Texas. End of story, right?

Well, if Jim had been writing this story, it would have been over. But God was writing it, and God used some of Jim's high school students to craft a different ending to Jim's biography.

You see, God's ways are not our ways (Isaiah 55:8). God allows us to reach for a dream, to experience the birth of a vision. But then, strangely, God allows that dream to die before it gets resurrected supernaturally. It's God's way of helping us develop a dependence on him and not ourselves.

Take the case of Abraham, who had been told by God that he would be the father of a great nation, and that his descendants would be as numerous as the grains of sand on the seashore. This was a great dream, one that Abraham longed to see fulfilled. But the dream slowly died as Abraham and his wife Sarah grew old. At one point, Abraham tried to resurrect the dream on his own, with disastrous results (Genesis 16). But in God's time, the dream came true, and Sarah gave birth to a son, Isaac, even though her biological clock had stopped ticking long before.

Or consider Joseph. He had a dream of being a great leader to whom many would bow down. But his dream was dashed on multiple occasions as he found himself thrown into a cistern and sold into slavery, or falsely accused by his employer's wife, or rotting in a jail cell. When it was obvious that Joseph could not make the dream come true on his own, God stepped in and resurrected the dream, promoting Joseph to the highest position in the land under Pharaoh, causing many to bow down before him.

The baseball program at Reagan County High School was small and underfunded, but Jim Morris kick-started the program and developed a winning attitude among the boys. In 1999 he challenged them to reach out and take hold of their dream of winning the district championship. They responded that they would if Jim would rekindle his old dream of playing major league baseball. Morris, by this time in his mid-30s, reluctantly agreed, and when the team won their district, Morris suddenly found himself at a Tampa Bay Devil Rays tryout camp, explaining to the scout that he had to keep his end of a bargain.

"I did it as a lark," remembers Jim, who is now a motivational speaker. "I thought I was going to embarrass myself."[1] With his kids in tow, Morris changed a diaper and then hustled out onto the field with players nearly half his age. While not initially interested in Morris, the scout allowed him to take a few tosses. Jim threw twelve consecutive fastballs clocked at 98 mph. Thirty-five-year-olds with surgical scars on their arms aren't supposed to be able to throw 88 mph, much less 98 mph. His family came around to the idea of dad being gone for the season, and before long, Morris was pitching AA baseball for Orlando.

He didn't stop there. After seeing what he could do, the team quickly promoted him to their AAA team in Durham. By September there was no stopping the Morris Express, and Jim was promoted to the big leagues with Tampa Bay. On September 19, 1999, thirty-five-year-old Jim Morris made his major-league debut, striking out the first batter he faced on four pitches.

Morris now credits God with orchestrating his path. "God has a funny way of bringing some things around and knocking you in the head with the ultimate destination," says the man whose dream was eventually turned into a Disney movie. "Something I should have achieved quite easily took me a long time to get around to. It came in His time, not mine."[2]

Jesus reminded his disciples that a seed must die before it germinates and produces a harvest. In a similar way, death to self will allow

God's true vision for our lives to be realized rather than our self-centered dreams.

Do you have a dream for your life, a God-given purpose that you feel you've been created for? God equips each of us to visualize what he intends to do in our lives. But when the dream dies, that's where hope kicks in. Hope is simply a way of anticipating that God is still at work in your life, even when the dream seems dead. Hope is expecting to see God work out his will for your life even when it doesn't seem possible.

And it's during that time of waiting that God is doing his greatest work: building your character. While you're developing qualities such as patience, faith, self-control, and other fruits of the Spirit, God is preparing you for even greater things than you can imagine when he does fulfill the vision.

Just ask Jim Morris, who is allowing the end of his story to be rewritten daily by God.

intentional walk: Lord God, so often I try to run ahead of you and fulfill my dreams on my own. I need your dreams, your visions for my life. Help me to soar high and dream your big dreams rather than be chained down by my small ones. And when the dream dies, may I open my heart and trust that you are still at work in my life, and that you will supernaturally bring your vision for my life to pass.

second

That one error fills him with faults.
—Proteus, in *The Two Gentlemen of Verona*, by William Shakespeare

If baseball is a game of inches generally speaking,
then it follows that it is specifically a game of split-seconds
for second basemen. There is no position on a
baseball team which places such a high premium on timing.
—Bobby Richardson, legendary Yankees second baseman

Just as man is destined to die once, and after that to
face judgment, so Christ was sacrificed once to take
away the sins of many people; and he will
appear a second time, not to bear sin, but to bring
salvation to those who are waiting for him.
—Hebrews 9:27-28

hear here

When the people saw the thunder and lightning and heard
the trumpet and saw the mountain in smoke, they trembled with fear.
They stayed at a distance and said to Moses, "Speak to us yourself
and we will listen. But do not have God speak to us or we will die."
Moses said to the people, "Do not be afraid. God has come to test
you, so that the fear of God will be with you to keep you from
sinning." The people remained at a distance, while Moses
approached the thick darkness where God was.

—Exodus 20:18-21

The most famous of the Dodger fans…was named Hilda Chester,
a plump, pink-faced woman with a mop of stringy
gray hair.…During the games Hilda lived in the bleacher

seats with her bell....With her fish peddler voice, she'd say,
"You know me. Hilda wit da bell. Ain't it trillin'? Home wuz
never like dis, mac." When disturbed her favorite
line was, "Eacha heart out, ya bum."
—Peter Golenbock, in *Bums: An Oral History of the Brooklyn Dodgers* (1984)

The sound track of a ballpark is very satisfying for most fans. In fact, there is a certain "all is right with the world" feeling when we hear the crack of the bat, the pop of the ball in a glove, and the umpire's voice yelling, "Safe!" above a roaring crowd. Even the nasal-voiced hot dog vendor roaming through the stands can go toe-to-toe with talented vocalists of our day.

But what if you couldn't hear any of that? Would it still be baseball?

Late in the 1993 season, when minor-leaguers are called up to the big leagues for a cup of coffee, an outfielder by the name of Curtis Pride made his debut with the Montreal Expos. The second-place Expos were at home, battling the Philadelphia Phillies for the division lead, when Pride stepped to the plate with the home team down 7–4 and two men on base.

He wasted no time, ripping a double on the first pitch that scored both runners. The capacity crowd of Olympic Stadium nearly brought the house down with their cheers for the young rookie. Time was called, and the Expos third base coach ran out to second base, but instead of congratulating Pride, the coach asked Pride to take off his helmet.

"What's wrong with my helmet?" wondered Pride.[1] Then he understood that third base coach Jerry Manuel wanted him to tip his helmet to the fans and acknowledge their cheers. Pride obliged, only then realizing that the people were thundering their applause for him.

You see, Curtis Pride is deaf. He can't hear the crack of the bat or most of the other sounds that we associate with baseball. With only 5 percent of his hearing intact due to his mother contracting rubella during her pregnancy, Pride has to read lips and sense vibrations from loud noises. But he communicates quite well and has vowed never to allow his disability to slow down his baseball career. "My other senses are more sensitive," he says. "Smell, feel, and seeing are much sharper because of my [lack of] hearing."[2]

After the game, a reporter asked Pride if he could hear the cheering, standing on second base. "Here," Pride said as he pointed to his heart. "I could hear it here."

How do you hear God speak? There have been many times that I wished I could hear God speak to me audibly to give me direction. Sometimes I think it would be great to simply surf over to www.willofGod.com so that I could understand what God is saying. Or maybe God would just arrange the clouds into letters and spell out his plans for my life. I would even take a text message on my cell phone from God.

But those are all methods of communicating from the outside in. Instead, God has put the Holy Spirit in our hearts to speak to us from the inside out, so that we might develop other spiritual senses—a growing faith, the mind of Christ, conviction, a persevering heart, a spirit that bears witness with another Christlike spirit.

To hear God speak is not like picking up the phone and hearing some mindless chatter from someone. God doesn't speak just for the sake of hearing his own voice. Instead, God speaks with the intent of moving us into action, to produce change in our lives. Maybe that's why a lot of Christians don't really listen to God. They don't really want to change. "You speak to us, Moses [or pastor or Sunday school teacher or famous TV preacher], and we will listen. But don't expect us to get into God's Word this week so that we might hear *God* speak to us. We're afraid that if we hear God speak to us, we will surely die."

Never were truer words spoken. To hear God speak will cost us dearly. To hear God speak, we must die to our self-centered nature, die to the noisy chatter of the world, and desire to obey whatever we hear. And many churchgoing people simply are unwilling to do that.

On the other hand, maybe real life doesn't begin until you hear God speak. For to hear God speak in your heart is the most satisfying sound of all.

intentional walk: Lord, I want to hear you speak. But there are so many other voices competing for bandwidth in my brain that I struggle to know which one is yours. I want to silence the competing signals that I receive from the media around me and to listen intently for your unmistakable voice above the chatter of the world. Help me take off my helmet today, that I might hear your voice and sense the applause of heaven when I act upon your Word.

no shortcuts

Do not let your heart envy sinners,
but always be zealous for the fear of the LORD.
There is surely a future hope for you,
and your hope will not be cut off.
—Proverbs 23:17-18

Greaseball, greaseball, greaseball.
That's all I throw him,
and he still hits them. He's the only player in
baseball who consistently hits my grease.
He sees the ball so well;
I guess he can pick out the dry side.
—Pitcher Gaylord Perry on batting champion Rod Carew

You name it, and over the years someone in baseball has tried it in order to get ahead.

Back in the early days of the game, when there was only one umpire, it was fairly common for a batter on first base to cut across the diamond to third when the ump wasn't looking. Infielders would retaliate by grabbing the belt of a legitimate base runner and delay him a few seconds on the base paths.

Pitchers have always tried to gain an advantage. For decades, it was normal practice for a pitcher to throw the spitball. And since the practice of using a fresh ball often in the game hadn't yet developed, by the late innings the ball would be dark with all sorts of foreign substances, making it difficult (and dangerous) for batters. That changed beginning in 1920. Teams were allowed a grandfather clause in which they could designate two hurlers on each roster to continue to throw a spitter. The last "legal" spitball pitcher, Burleigh Grimes, retired in 1934.

But through the decades that followed, some pitchers must have been going to medical school on the side, they doctored the ball up so much. Gaylord Perry was suspected of throwing a ball loaded with Vaseline and is one of the few players in the postmodern era to be suspended for throwing illegal pitches. Perry had an elaborate routine before every pitch, touching his cap, his belt, his ears, his jersey, his knees, and everything but the scoreboard before he threw the ball. In this way, he was trying to get inside the mind of the hitter and send the message that he might be throwing a loaded ball. Customs officials and security personnel today would have a field day with Perry, who liked to hide a foreign substance all over his body and dare the umpires to find it. Gene Tenace, Perry's catcher with the Padres, once said that sometimes the ball was so loaded he couldn't throw it back to the mound.

Other pitchers tried scuffing the ball. Whitey Ford and Don Sutton were both accused of this. Joe Niekro was once confronted on the mound by umpires who wanted to see what was in his pocket. Niekro pulled his hand out of his back pocket, and an emery board popped out and landed a few feet from the mound. Joe looked like the cat that swallowed the canary, and he said that he used the board to file his nails between innings. The league office didn't believe that his nails could grow so fast, so they suspended him for ten games.

And of course, batters have occasionally honored the age-old saying "If you're not cheating, you're not trying." Norm Cash admitted to using a corked bat in his monster season of 1961, when he led the league with a .361 batting average, a mark that he never came close to again in his career. Others have gone to the plate with sawdust, styrofoam, or superballs hidden in the hollow of their bat, trying to gain just a little more bat speed and enjoy a little more success.

Batters have always tried to pick up signs of what pitch might be coming next, but some teams have gone to extraordinary means to relay that kind of information to a hitter. In 1951 the Giants came from 13½ games behind in August to beat the Dodgers for the pennant. Many years later, it was confirmed by some of the Giants that they had a coach who sat in the clubhouse, just beyond center field at the old Polo Grounds, and used a telescope to steal the signs that the opposing catcher was giving to the pitcher. He would then set off a buzzer system in the dugout that signaled what kind of pitch was coming next, and then a relay man signaled the batter at the plate.

Illicit drugs have often been found in the clubhouse. Amphetamines, known as "greenies," were common in clubhouses in the 1960s and 1970s. But the steroid and HGH scandal of the last twenty years has created a stench in the sport as some of baseball's most hallowed records have fallen. Records from the steroid era will always be suspect. And in stark contrast to all these cheaters stands Al Worthington.

Al had a fine career as a pitcher with several teams. As a starter with the Giants in the 1950s, he threw complete game shutouts in the first two games he appeared in. And he was a dominant closer for the Twins in the 1960s, playing a key role in their 1965 pennant-winning season. But in 1960 Al was traded to the White Sox, and he had been with the team only a few days when his troubles began.

"One of the pitchers told me that we had a man in the scoreboard with binoculars who was stealing the signs of the opposing team's catcher," Al remembers. "He would then send what the pitcher was throwing to the batter by way of a light in the scoreboard. If it was going to be a curveball, the light would flash on and off. If it was going to be a fastball, the light stayed on."

Al had no problem with stealing signs on the field, believing that to be just part of the game. But he did have a problem with binoculars and lights on the scoreboard. "I like to win, but I don't want to win if I have to cheat to do it. A couple more days went by, and then I went to the manager, Al Lopez. I told him it was cheating and that I couldn't play with a team that cheats."[1]

Worthington had become a Christian in 1958 after hearing the gospel at a Billy Graham crusade, and he began to take very seriously the call to obey Christ in every part of his life. When the White Sox front office refused to do away with the elaborate sign-stealing scheme, Worthington retired from baseball, and he was out of baseball for two years before being picked up by the Reds in 1963. He retired from baseball in 1969, and only recently did he retire from his second career as a minister and missionary.

Had there been baseball in biblical times, there probably would have been cheating then as well, for the root cause of cheating is envy, one of the seven deadly sins. Envy is what takes over when we want what someone else has but don't want to put in the honest effort or take the time to acquire it legitimately. Instead, we look for a short-cut to success.

Cain envied Abel's relationship with God and eventually killed his brother (Genesis 4:2-8). Joseph's brothers resented the favoritism that their father showed him, so they sold him into slavery (Genesis 37:3-28). Saul was jealous of the praise that David received (1 Samuel 18:8-9). Pilate knew that the Jewish religious leaders trumped up the charges against Jesus because they envied his popularity with the people (Mark 15:9-11).

The problem with envy is that it really doesn't get for us what we want. Instead, it gives us more of the same emptiness.

Instead of being envious, the writer of Proverbs tells us, we are to be "zealous for the fear of the LORD"—in other words, to have a personal focus on a right relationship with God. God's plans for you are different from his plans for someone else. You may be filled with envy toward a teammate who has hit so many home runs. Or you might envy a coworker who received a promotion that you had wanted. Maybe envy a neighbor who seems to have more "toys" than you do.

But God does have a future hope for you, and he promises that it will not be cut off. What if God's plans for you are to bring you even more success than the person you are envying? You might miss it if you're not pursuing a right relationship with God.

intentional walk: Lord, sometimes I don't like it when other people experience success and I don't. It hurts when I see them achieve something that I wanted for myself. I guess that my heart has got a long way to go before I totally trust your plans for my life. Help me to seek you first above all things (Matthew 6:33), knowing that your plans for my life are the best and are greater than any plans that I could come up with on my own.

lefty's blaze

"In your anger do not sin": Do not let the sun go down while you are still angry, and do not give the devil a foothold....Do not let any unwholesome talk come out of your mouths, but only what is helpful for building others up according to their needs, that it may benefit those who listen. And do not grieve the Holy Spirit of God, with whom you were sealed for the day of redemption. Get rid of all bitterness, rage and anger, brawling and slander, along with every form of malice. Be kind and compassionate to one another, forgiving each other, just as in Christ God forgave you.

—Ephesians 4:26-27, 29-32

He could throw a lamb chop past a wolf.

—Westbrook Pegler on pitcher Lefty Grove

He won twenty or more games seven times in a row, and nine ERA titles. He could strike out the side on nine pitches, and he did it more than once in the same season. He once won sixteen games in a row, and he won exactly three hundred in his lifetime. Over the course of parts of two seasons, he was an incredible 46–4, the best fifty-game stretch by any pitcher in baseball history. And when his career was almost done, he reinvented himself as a relief pitcher, leading the league in saves because he could control the strike zone so well. Unfortunately, he couldn't control his temper.

Robert Moses "Lefty" Grove, arguably baseball's greatest left-handed pitcher, had a blazing fastball and a hot temper to match. While he was leading the league in wins and ERA year after year, he also led the league in destruction of private property. When things weren't going his way, he kicked water buckets, ripped his uniform, and caused teammates to run for cover as he smashed up the locker room. He so assumed that others struggled with the same problem that he once handed out this piece of advice: "Kid," he advised one rookie, "when you kick a water bucket never kick it with your toes. Always use the side of your foot."[1]

In 1931 Grove and his Philadelphia A's were on top of the world. The A's were headed to their third straight World Series appearance, and Grove had won sixteen games in a row. And on August 23, 1931, going up against the hapless St. Louis Browns, it looked like the seventeenth win in a row was in the bag.

But future Hall of Fame outfielder Al Simmons was not in the A's line-up that day, having left town to go to a doctor's appointment. In his place was rookie Jimmy Moore, and Moore must have wondered after the game if he would ever get another chance in the big leagues. Moore misjudged a fly ball that allowed the Browns to score the only run of the game, and Grove and the A's lost 1–0. The highly competitive Grove returned to the clubhouse and proceeded to destroy everything in sight, cursing Simmons, Moore, and anyone else within earshot. He shot his mouth off at the team for only managing three hits in the game. He was even angry at manager Connie Mack for allowing Simmons to be out of the lineup.

But Mack, known for his patience and optimism, saw things differently. "Robert, didn't Coffman [Browns pitcher] pitch a wonderful game? We made only three hits and we wouldn't have scored a run if we'd been still playing." Only when he heard the kind words of the highly respected Mack did Grove back down.[2]

A competitive spirit is one thing, but destructive anger is another. Former Reds pitcher Frank Pastore distinguishes between the two: "The psychological profile of an athlete closely resembles that of a fighter pilot. They both must have a purposeful passion, but not an out of control anger that will mess up your concentration or otherwise get you off your game. If you carry that kind of anger, your opponent has already won. This is not the right way to approach competition. Don't try to destroy the enemy. Instead, seek a personal best; seek your own personal excellence. This is what allows a Christian to be a boxer, or an offensive lineman in football, for instance. It is not a destructive anger they carry into the game, but a controlled passion that helps them achieve their personal best."[3]

Pastor Andy Stanley has a healthy perspective on anger: "We need to admit that we all get angry. Anger is actually part of what it is to be human. When injustice occurs in our life, anger is produced. Don't try to sound spiritual and say, 'I'm not going to be angry.' Instead, go ahead and admit your pain. It's ok to feel angry, but it's not ok to do just anything about it. We can't afford to let our anger control our actions. There are the feelings produced by anger, and then the sinful decisions produced by anger. We need to be able to split the two apart."[4]

Paul also cautions us to deal with anger as soon as possible. "Do not let the sun go down on your anger," he wrote. It's easy to let the embers of anger smolder and grow hotter and hotter as we steam over how we've been wronged. The reason Paul cautions us about anger is that he knows its great potential to lead us into sin.

As Christians, we really only have two options when we're angry. We must either lovingly confront the person who has offended us or lovingly overlook the offense (Proverbs 19:11). To refuse both of these choices is to choose to hold on to our anger and, in effect, to give the devil a foothold in our lives.

In Galatians 5:19-21 Paul lists the acts of the sinful nature. You would expect such things as sexual immorality, witchcraft, and drunkenness to make the list. But right there, in the middle of idolatry and orgies, he lists "fits of rage." Why do we so easily dismiss our unrighteous anger? A pastor who was found guilty of any of the other things on the list would be asked to resign immediately. But somehow, we tend to overlook a hot temper and excuse it as something that's just part of our nature.

Things will happen in life that are beyond your control. Other people will drop the ball. Your record won't be spotless, either. But to choose anger over forgiveness is to say to our enemy, "Satan, come on into my heart. Come take control and work your way through my life and my relationships." You might protest, "I would never do that." But if you are harboring anger and unforgiveness toward someone, you already have.

So, how do you forgive others? Paul says to forgive them as God forgave you. And how did God forgive you? God forgave you ahead of time. God went to the cross, knowing that a couple of thousand years later, you would sin and need a Savior. God chose to forgive you before you ever sinned. We live in a state of forgiveness before God, so we must allow others to live in a state of forgiveness before us. The way to deal with your anger quickly is to decide to forgive in advance those who will hurt you.

intentional walk: Lord, I thank you that my sins are forgiven. And I know that sometime soon a person will cross my path, a person with whom I have issues of anger and unforgiveness. Just as I believe by faith that you have forgiven me, so by faith I choose to forgive that person today, in advance, for anything that he or she has done or ever will do to me. By your grace, God, help me to keep no record of wrongs of other people (1 Corinthians 13:5).

eyes on the prize

Not that I have already obtained all this, or have already
been made perfect, but I press on to take hold of
that for which Christ Jesus took hold of me.
Brothers, I do not consider myself
yet to have taken hold of it. But one thing I do:
Forgetting what is behind and straining toward what is ahead,
I press on toward the goal to win the prize for which
God has called me heavenward in Christ Jesus.
—Philippians 3:12-14

There ain't no Hotel Episode in Detroit.
—Rube Waddell, after being fined by his manager,
who was upset about "that disgraceful hotel episode in Detroit."

His real name was George Edward Waddell, but everyone called him *Rube*, which, like *hick* or *bumpkin*, was a common nickname for an unsophisticated player from the sticks. And George Edward lived up to his name from the moment he was born, on Friday the thirteenth, to the moment he passed away, on April Fools Day. Waddell was an eccentric clown who was baseball's original "man child," a great athletic specimen who had the emotional makeup of a little boy.

But my, oh my, when he had the inclination, he could pitch—that is, when he was focused. Waddell held the National League record for strikeouts by a lefty for sixty-one years before Sandy Koufax broke his mark of 349 Ks. He led the league in strikeouts six years in a row, and he also won twenty games four years in a row. Once, against the Tigers, he ordered his outfielders to move in, and then he proceeded to strike out the side.

But if ever there was an adult case of ADD (attention deficit disorder), Waddell had it.

Take the year 1903, for example. Rube won twenty-two games for the Philadelphia A's, played rugby for a Michigan team, performed in a play called *The Stain of Guilt*, married and separated from his second wife, wrestled with alligators, saved a woman from drowning, accidentally shot a friend through the hand, and was bitten by a lion.

Hall of Famer Sam Crawford said of Waddell, "Rube was one of a kind—just a big kid, you know. He'd pitch one day and we wouldn't see him for three or four days after. He'd just disappear, go fishing or something, or be off playing ball with a bunch of twelve-year-olds in an empty lot somewhere. You couldn't control him 'cause he was just a big kid himself. Baseball was just a game to Rube."[1]

Once a game was delayed because starting pitcher Waddell was nowhere to be found. Finally, he was seen playing marbles under the stands with a group of children. Then there was the time management tried to curtail his impulsive spending habits by paying his year's salary of $2,200 in one-dollar bills, little by little. In another instance, he pitched both games of a doubleheader just so that he could get a few days off to go fishing.

Rube was fascinated by fire engines. On more than one occasion, he was on the mound, heard the clanging of the fire bell, and left the ballpark in the middle of the game to chase the fire engine and try to assist with the blaze. He often wore a red undershirt so that he could strip off his uniform top and look like just another firefighter at the scene.

And if no fire engines happened to pass by, members of the opposing team would do their best to fluster Rube. Often a first base coach from the opposing team took some props onto the field. Facing the left-handed Waddell on the mound, coaches would pull out a rubber snake, a jack-in-the-box, or a child's stuffed animal and wave it to distract the big southpaw.

The sad thing about Waddell is what might have been. Blessed with a gifted left arm, but cursed with a propensity for strong drink, Waddell won "only" 193 games in a career and a life shortened by alcohol. He died at the age of thirty-seven in a sanitarium in San Antonio.

What's the biggest distraction that you face daily? What gets your life off course quicker than a Rube Waddell fastball? Well, there certainly are conflicting messages in the media that we expose ourselves to. But in Philippians 3, the apostle Paul talks about another distraction that affects everyone—the past.

"Forgetting everything that is behind" was the way Paul put it. And he certainly had a lot to forget. Paul carried more baggage than a cruise ship. Before his experience on the Damascus road, he had persecuted the church, hauling its members off to jail and supervising the execution of its leaders. He even referred to himself as the worst of sinners (1 Timothy 1:15).

What gives you more problems: trying to remember the things you forget, or trying to forget the things you remember?

All of us have baggage. And Satan constantly accuses us and belittles us, reminding us about our past failures and sins. In fact, his major tactic in your life is to harass you by accusing you. But it won't last forever. The next time Satan reminds you about your past, just remind him about his future: "Then I heard a loud voice in heaven say: 'Now have come the salvation and the power and the kingdom of our God, and the authority of his Christ. For the accuser of our brothers, who accuses them before our God day and night, has been hurled down'" (Revelation 12:10).

Does your past distract you from serving God in the present or hoping for a glorious future? Press on. You may never forget the facts about the past, but if you keep your eyes on Jesus, he can help you forget the sting of the past. A prize awaits you if you keep your eyes focused on the finish line. Your Savior is waiting for you to finish this life strong, and the multitudes who have played the game of life before you are cheering you on from the stands. Press on.

intentional walk: Heavenly Father, sometimes I feel crippled by my past sins and mistakes. I give you my shame-filled memories and painful remembrances, and even though I can't forget the facts about them, I ask that you would remove the sting of these memories. Help me to fill those empty places in my heart and mind with new memories of intentionally walking with you.

the pitch that changed everything

Be careful to follow every command I am giving you today,
so that you may live and increase and may enter and possess
the land that the LORD promised on oath to your forefathers.
Remember how the LORD your God led you all the way
in the desert these forty years, to humble you and to test you
in order to know what was in your heart, whether or not you would
keep his commands. He humbled you, causing you to hunger and
then feeding you with manna, which neither you nor your fathers had
known, to teach you that man does not live on bread alone but on
every word that comes from the mouth of the LORD.

—Deuteronomy 8:1-3

Anytime you think you have the game conquered,
the game will turn around and punch you right in the nose.
—Mike Schmidt, Phillies Hall of Fame third baseman

For Frank Pastore, success was easy and came early in life. Whether it was being elected senior class president in high school and dating a popular cheerleader, or being offered an academic scholarship to Stanford, or receiving the largest signing bonus in Reds history at that time, Pastore was on top of the world as a seventeen-year-old.

And in due time that success followed him to the majors, where he made his debut on opening day of the season in 1979, coming into the game in relief of his boyhood idol, Tom Seaver. With a wink from catcher Johnny Bench and encouraging words from the manager, Pastore reared back and threw as hard as he could, struck out the hitters, and got his team out of trouble.

Back in the locker room, Pastore continued to celebrate as he was congratulated by his teammates. Then his venerable catcher called him over to his locker. "Kid," Bench said prophetically, "there's two things you need to know about playing in the major leagues. First, it's harder to stay here than it is to get here. And second, never get too cocky or too arrogant, because you're always only one pitch away from humility."[1]

Those are great words to live by. If only Frank had listened.

Over the course of the next several years, Pastore enjoyed some success with the Reds. Unfortunately, this wasn't the Big Red Machine of the 1970s, so Frank and the other Reds pitchers often had little run support. The team was up and down in the standings but never enjoyed the success of the 1970s team that had been led by so many future Hall of Famers.

But Pastore didn't allow the team's lack of outward success to curtail his own signs of upward mobility and importance. Sporting the lavish house, the extravagant cars, and a beautiful wife, Pastore had seemingly everything to live for—except God. Frank considered himself to be a practicing atheist, as he doubted the existence of God. His simply philosophy was "He who dies with the most toys wins," and he believed that he could create his own happiness if he became rich and famous.

Then in June of 1984 the words of the prophet Bench came true. Pastore was pitching against the Dodgers in Los Angeles, enjoying a 3–1 lead in the eighth inning, when his career—not to mention his worldview—came crashing down around him. On a 2–2 pitch, Dodger infielder Steve Sax rifled the fastball back through the box, and Pastore couldn't get out of its way. The ball ricocheted off his pitching elbow into the outfield, and even as he was falling to the mound in intense pain, Frank knew that his life would never be the same. Ironically, as he was being helped off the field, this atheist was praying, "Why, God, why?"

But it was during his stint on the disabled list that Frank began to get some different perspective. Tom Hume, the Reds chapel leader, invited Frank to begin attending a Bible study for some of the guys on the team. With nothing better to do, and believing that he could easily disarm those who believed in the Bible and the God it spoke of, Frank went to the meeting. It didn't take long before he passionately dumped his anger and frustration on the guys in attendance, attacking Christianity and anyone who would believe its premises. But the guys in the study didn't seem to be offended. Instead, they accepted Frank as he was and encouraged him to pursue some of his own study of the Bible in order to disprove it and to prove his humanistic worldview.

Frank eagerly took on the challenge, since he had plenty of time to read and reflect. Over the course of the next several days and weeks, he would sneak off to read books on apologetics that the guys had given him. The reality of God's existence and love for Frank began to dawn on him. Finally, in a clubhouse in Pittsburgh, Frank had his epiphany, and he simply whispered a confession: "Jesus, you're alive!" He gave his heart and mind to the Savior that day, and he began a journey of faith that has led him into ministry and allowed him to impact the lives of countless numbers of people for the sake of Christ.[2]

But it all began when he realized that he had been only one pitch away from humility all the time. And even though the vast majority of us aren't and never will be major league pitchers, all of us are all only one pitch away from humility as well.

What about those difficult seasons in life? You know, the ones where we're tempted to have a pity party or get angry and ask the same question that Frank asked: "Why, God, why?" Those seasons are not proof that God has abandoned us; quite the opposite, they are evidence of God's presence in our lives. God is testing us during those times because he wants to see—and more importantly, wants us to see—what is in our hearts.

It's during those times that God humbles us to help us develop a dependence on him alone. When all those props in life that we've cherished begin to fail, it's so that we might see that God will never fail. In fact, we could say that trials are proof of God's love. God loves us so much that he won't let us remain the way we are, drifting aimlessly without a Savior.

intentional walk: Loving God, you are a Father who disciplines his children, and I admit that sometimes I get too big for my britches and begin to rely on my abilities rather than on yours. How patient you are, God, to use even pain and struggles in my life to slowly woo me away from the world, with its empty philosophies of life, and captivate me with the beauty of your truth. Forgive me for the times when I blame you for the difficult circumstances that I am in. May the trials that I go through each day serve to be stepping-stones for a new life of utter dependence on you for everything.

names

So Jacob was left alone, and a man wrestled with
him till daybreak. When the man saw that he could not overpower
him, he touched the socket of Jacob's hip so that his hip
was wrenched as he wrestled with the man.
Then the man said, "Let me go, for it is daybreak."
But Jacob replied, "I will not let you go unless you bless me."
The man asked him, "What is your name?"
"Jacob," he answered.
Then the man said, "Your name will no longer
be Jacob, but Israel, because you have
struggled with God and with men
and have overcome."

—Genesis 32:24-28

I was pitching in the minors and all of a sudden it
started to pour. I saw this awning in center field and
started to run under it. The only trouble was the
awning was painted on the wall.
From then on I was Dizzy.

—Paul "Dizzy" Trout, recalling the origin of his nickname

In the introduction I mentioned my namesakes, my father and my grandfather, and also the Hugh Poland who caught for four teams in five years
in the 1940s. His best moment was when he and another player were
traded for National League MVP and Hall of Fame catcher Ernie
"Schnozz" Lombardi. Lombardi's nickname suggests that his nose was
as big as his batting average, which was a lifetime .305.

Speaking of nicknames, give me those names of yesteryear. They told
you so much about the player. Some sobriquets, like Ernie "Schnozz"
Lombardi, described the person's physical characteristics. You can guess
what made "Specs" Toporcer, or Mordecai "Three Finger" Brown
famous. I guess "Bones" Ely and "Fat Freddie" Fitzsimmons would
have made an interesting pair if they had been on the same team. And
with "Piano Legs" Hickman and "No Neck" Williams, I suppose you
have the long and the short of it all.

Other handles that players wore described their personalities. There was "Cool Papa" Bell, Al "The Mad Hungarian" Hrabosky, "Sad" Sam Jones, and more Rubes and Babes than you can count. And who could forget brothers "Dizzy" and "Daffy" Dean?

It would be pretty easy to field an all-food-and-beverage team. Try ordering from a menu of George "Pea Soup" Dumont for an appetizer and a main course of Fred "Chicken" Stanley, Frank "Noodles" Hahn, and Harry "Beans" Keener. You could wash it down with Gene "Half Pint" Rye (who once homered three times in one inning in the minors) and enjoy Willie "Puddin' Head" Jones for dessert.

The animal kingdom is also represented well among nicknames in baseball lore. You could have some real sluggers in your lineup, such as Roy "Squirrel" Sievers, Norm "Turkey" Stearns, and the "Red Rooster," Doug Radar. But those might be small prey for the carnivores such as Lance "Big Puma" Berkman, Ron "Gator" Guidry, and "The Big Cat," Johnny Mize.

Some nicknames are just plain intriguing: Oil Can Boyd; Bow Wow Arft; The Meal Ticket; The Mechanical Man; Scrap Iron.

Nicknames are interesting because they tell us something about another person. In Scripture a name often signified a particular character quality about a person. That's why it's so important to learn and understand the many names of God. By getting to know God's names and what they mean, we learn more about what God is like, what his character qualities and traits are.

Our names mean something too, and this lesson wasn't lost on the patriarch Jacob. Ol' Jake came out of the womb scrapping with his brother, and so he was named "Jacob," which literally means "heel grabber." We would translate it as "deceiver" or "supplanter." He lived up to his name, all right. He supplanted his older brother, Esau, as the one in the family who would receive the birthright, tricking his brother into giving up title to the assets of their father, Isaac. Later, spurred on by his devious mother, Rebekah, Jacob took the place of his brother and stole the blessing from his father as well.

Jacob was shrewd in business as well, and he schemed against his uncle Laban to build up his flocks of sheep and goats. But over time he used enough people in enough places that it caught up with him, and he found himself on the run, looking over his shoulder for the sight of anyone who had a long memory of dealing with his selfish ways.

Finally, in Genesis 32, Jacob found himself at a physical and spiritual crossroads. He got alone with God and wrestled with the angel of God all night long. When the angel asked him, "What is your name?" it wasn't because God had forgotten what to call Jacob. Instead, the mysterious being was asking for a confession from Jacob. "What is your character? What are you truly like?" asked the angel. And for once, Jacob didn't look for an excuse by blaming it on his conniving mother or his swindling uncle.

"My name is Jacob," the patriarch finally answered. "I am a heel-grabber, a deceiver. This is my true character."

And when Jacob finally owned up to his past, his confession set him free, and God bestowed a new name on him. "Your name will no longer be called Jacob," said the angel, "but Israel, because you have struggled with God and with men and have overcome." When Jacob confessed his sinful nature, God bestowed a new nature on him: Israel, one who struggles and strives to be with God.

But it's interesting to note that when Jacob asked the angel what *his* name was, the being would not answer. In those days, to know someone's name suggested that you had a kind of power over them. By not revealing his name to Jacob at that time, it was as if God was saying, "No, Jacob, you will not rule over me. My power is not for sale, and you'll not be able to harness it for your own selfish interests."

Admitting our sin and weakness is never easy. It cost Jacob his pride to go the distance with God that night. And as the sun began to come up, the venerable patriarch found himself limping because his hip was injured in the midnight wrestling match. But even though his physical life suffered, his spirit grew mighty, for Israel limping is always better than Jacob walking.

intentional walk: What is my name? Reveal to me, Lord, the depth of my character, and transform me into one who can wear the name "Christian" in a worthy manner. Not that I could ever be worthy on my own to bear your name, but I pray that you might bestow on me the goodness and virtue that my character lacks. May I always learn more about your name, not to somehow control you (as if I ever could!), but rather that I might see the depth of your greatness and majesty.

third

Look to the plate.

—First Servant, in *Romeo and Juliet*, by William Shakespeare

Third ain't so bad if nothin' is hit to you.

—Catcher Yogi Berra on Casey Stengel's experiment using him as a third baseman

"Sir," they said, "we remember that while he was still alive that deceiver said, 'After three days I will rise again.' So give the order for the tomb to be made secure until the third day. Otherwise, his disciples may come and steal the body and tell the people that he has been raised from the dead. This last deception will be worse than the first." "Take a guard," Pilate answered. "Go, make the tomb as secure as you know how."

—Matthew 27:63-65

crossing the line

No temptation has seized you except
what is common to man.
And God is faithful; he will not let you be
tempted beyond what you can bear. But when you
are tempted, he will also provide a way out so
that you can stand up under it.
—1 Corinthians 10:13

The easiest thing in sports is to win when you're good.
The next easiest is to lose when you're not any good.
The hardest—way hardest—is to lose
when you're good. That's the test of character.
—Roy Eisenhardt, former Oakland A's owner

To begin with, Willie Mays Aikens wants to debunk the myth that he was named after Hall of Famer Willie "Say Hey" Mays. He now goes simply by "Willie" and signs his name "Willie M. Aikens."

"My uncle's name was Willie, and there was a Dr. Mays that worked in the neighborhood," explained the former World Series hero from his Atlanta Federal Penitentiary cell.

He also wanted to debunk the idea that being incarcerated since 1994 was totally wrong and unjust. Willie, having come clean on his crime, added, "Being behind these walls for so many years is very sad and disappointing, but if I hadn't come to prison, then my life would have ended a long time ago. Praise the Lord!"

His was the life that many dream about. A three-sport athletic star at Seneca High School in South Carolina, Willie came up with the California Angels and stuck for good in 1979, when he belted twenty-one home runs. Then he was traded to the Kansas City Royals. He fit perfectly into their lineup and had his best year ever in 1980, driving in ninety-eight runs and helping lead his team to the World Series.

As the Royals faced the "Impossible Dream" Phillies in the fall classic, Willie came alive. He hit .400 for the series. He homered twice in the first game and twice in the fourth game, becoming the only player in World Series history to hit two home runs in the same game twice during the same World Series. But something else happened in that series, something that typified the way Willie lived life.

When Willie would come to the plate, he had a habit of digging in toward the back of the batter's box. Over the course of a game, he would blur the chalk line so much that his back foot would be on or over the line. "I would get as far back in the batter's box in order to catch the late break on the curveball," he explained.

In the fifth game, all that changed. Home plate umpire Dutch Rennert, a veteran National League arbiter, had seen enough. As Aikens stepped into the batter's box, Rennert took Willie's bat, put the handle on the ground, and drew a new back line in the dirt. As he handed the bat back to Willie, he smiled and said, "Step over that line and you'll be out."

Unfortunately, Willie had already crossed the line in his personal life. By 1993 the Royals star had experienced a royal downfall. He was out of baseball, addicted to cocaine, his body a shell of the star athlete he had been. He was arrested for selling small amounts of crack and, in a controversial move, was sentenced to prison for twenty-five years. Willie had gone from the big time to the big house.

When it comes to sin, God draws a line in the sand. Often we think that we can blur the line. We say that we don't mean to actually step over the line; we just want to get as close to the line as we can. But as the saying goes, "Sin will take you farther than you want to go, make you stay longer than you want to stay, and cost more than you can afford to pay." This certainly was true of Willie M. Aikens and it was true of King David, who experienced his own royal downfall.

King David had it all: position and power, riches, the adulation of the people, and a loving wife. Yet he allowed himself to be carried away by temptation in an affair with Bathsheba and the subsequent murder of her husband. You see, he blurred the lines of his power and stepped over into sin. What began as a thought in his mind created ripple effects throughout his lifetime and beyond, as the royal palace became a house of adultery, murder, lies, premature death, conspiracy, jealousy, and fear—all from getting too close to the line just once.

But through the tears of sorrow and shame, David repented. He was not just apologetic that he got caught, sorry for the consequences of his sin. David truly repented, realizing that he had sinned against God. Psalm 51 records the words of his prayer. Phrases such as "Have mercy on me, O God," "Against you, you only have I sinned," and "Create in me a clean heart, O God" don't sound like the typical confession of today's celebrities. Modern-day press conference confessionals are often delivered without any remorse, punctuated with sentences such as, "If I have offended anyone, I apologize," or "If anyone has misinterpreted my actions, I'm sorry."

In Willie's case, the prison sentence got his attention, and he truly repented, admitting that he was wrong. And then in prison, he rededicated his life to Christ. "I was highly favored by the Lord to have ever been a baseball player. God allowed me to be at the top of my profession, but then I destroyed it all by my drug use," Willie said from his cell, where he passed out Bibles to newcomers to the Atlanta Federal Penitentiary. "Not many people can say they have lived life at the top and at the bottom. But since being at the bottom, I have gained the most precious gift of all, eternal life through Christ."[1]

On June 4, 2008, Willie was released from prison under new federal guidelines for sentencing those convicted on drug charges. But he was already a free man because of what Christ had done in his heart while he was behind bars.

intentional walk: Lord Jesus, you were tempted in every way, just like I am. But you never gave in—not once (Hebrews 4:15). I'm thankful that you can identify with me at my point of temptation, because there is no temptation that you haven't seen or felt at some point in your earthly life. Be my way out today, before I cross the line.

the natural

See to it, brothers, that none of you has a sinful,
unbelieving heart that turns away from the living God.
But encourage one another daily, as long as it is called
Today, so that none of you may be hardened
by sin's deceitfulness.
—Hebrews 3:12-13

Baseball…can be a game, a pastime, or it can be
something by which we measure the seasons of our lives,
or it can be something that serves metaphorically
for the battles, the wars, the triumphs,
and the tragedies of any kind of human conflict.
—Daniel Okrent, American writer and editor

He looks more like a walking advertisement for a tattoo parlor than a ballplayer. And Josh Hamilton regrets that. But it's all part of history, part of *his story*, a part that he wouldn't want you to miss.

When Josh Hamilton was drafted by the Tampa Bay Devil Rays in 1999, it marked the beginning of a period in his life when "devil" was more than just the name of a baseball organization, as the tattoo on his left arm attests.

Hamilton was considered a fantastic five-tool prospect: he could hit, hit for power, run, throw, and field. He was given a huge signing bonus by Tampa Bay, which made him the first high school player to be the number-one draft choice in major league baseball since Alex Rodriguez in 1993.

Fast-forward to 2001. Josh and his parents were involved in a car accident, and they, whom he had leaned on during his minor league career, went back home to recover from injuries. Josh found himself alone for the first time in his life. Flush with loads of cash from his $4 million signing bonus and lots of free time, he began to hang out at a tattoo parlor. The friends that he made there led him to try alcohol and drugs, and he quickly found that he liked them.

Josh's on-field success left him as quickly as his signing bonus, which he was going through at an alarming rate to buy the cocaine that his body craved. He tried prayer and he tried rehab centers, but he continued to find himself caught in a downward spiral of highs and lows. Baseball gave up on him, and so did the drug dealers when his money ran out.

When Josh was at one of his lowest points, he paid a late-night visit to Michael Dean Chadwick, a home builder in Raleigh, who had battled the demons of drugs himself. Chadwick not only built houses for a living; he also was a faith-based motivational speaker who helped people build their homes and lives around Jesus. Chadwick began to help the tortured ballplayer, and he could see how seriously Josh wanted to change. Chadwick's daughter Katie also noticed, and it wasn't long before she and Josh fell in love and were married.

But the allure of the drugs was still too much for Josh, and the young couple began to have problems. Katie could have walked out on him, but she trusted that God would heal Josh and their marriage. "God told me he was going to give Josh baseball back, but it was not going to be for baseball," Katie says. "It was going to be for something much bigger. He was going to give Josh a platform to help others."[1]

In 2006, after a long stretch of sobriety, Josh was reinstated by Major League Baseball and began playing ball again at the lowest level in the minors. Then, the Cincinnati Reds took a chance on the young outfielder and discovered that his skills had not diminished. Hamilton started opening day with the Reds and played the entire year with them before being traded to the Texas Rangers, where he had a breakout season in 2008.

But there's one more person who is a key to Hamilton's success, and that is his personal coach, mentor, and accountability partner, Johnny Narron. Narron, a mature Christian, had coached Josh in a youth league years before, and he just happened to be a coach with the Reds when they acquired Hamilton. So part of Johnny's job was to befriend Josh and help hold him accountable every day for where he went, whom he was with, and what he did.

Since money is always a temptation for a recovering drug addict, Johnny carries Josh's meal money on the road. Free time and friends are also a temptation for Josh, so Johnny is his constant companion. And three times a week Narron makes sure that Josh passes his drug tests. "I think he looks forward to the tests," says Narron. He looks at those tests as a way to reassure people around him who had faith."[2]

It's true. Josh welcomes the accountability, because he knows he can't make it as a ballplayer, much less as a husband and father, without it. "If I ever get in a bad situation, I know I would have to get out of it and give Johnny a call," says Josh.

When Josh was traded to Texas, Narron went too, hired by the Rangers as a special-assignment coach. Hamilton goes nowhere without the man who has become part-time chaplain, part-time chaperone, and full-time friend. When Katie and the kids are gone, Narron stays at Hamilton's apartment. On the road, when other teammates are going out at night, Josh and Johnny stay in adjoining hotel rooms and have Bible study together.

"I'm there for Josh, always," says Johnny. "When he gets antsy, he'll come up to me and say, 'Let's do a devotional.'"[3] And one favorite verse of Josh's is James 4:7: "Submit yourselves, then, to God. Resist the devil, and he will flee from you."

"Encourage one another daily," said the writer of the book of Hebrews, "so that none of you will be hardened by sin's deceitfulness." Every Christian needs daily encouragement from another believer, someone who will challenge us to be our best. We all need to be in a position where we are answerable to someone for our actions. The truth is that we all have addictions. Some are just more socially acceptable than others. But all addictions force us to try to find life apart from Christ, and that's why even the smallest habits and innocent routines can be dangerous to our spirits. They can serve to convince us that we can find joy and pleasure in our lives without Jesus.

So who are you when no one else is around? Josh Hamilton found out the hard way that living on your own, without accountability, will lead you down the wrong road. But with a team of accountability partners in Jerry Narron, Michael Chadwick, and Katie, Josh has begun to realize his potential again—not simply to be a good ballplayer, but to make his life count for Christ.

"My mission is to be the ray of hope, the guy who stands out there on that beautiful field and owns up to his mistakes and lets people know it's never completely hopeless, no matter how bad it seems at the time," says Josh, reflecting on the changes that God has brought into his life.[4]

The tattoos on his arms now help the messenger tell the story of God's grace. They serve not just as reminders of his painful past; they also are evidence of the greatness of God's love.

intentional walk: Jesus, friend of sinners, help me to humble myself before you. I thank you that you provide accountability partners, people to encourage me and challenge me in my walk with you. Help me to embrace them as messengers whom you have put in my life to help me become all I can be.

no "i" in team

I wrote to the church, but Diotrephes, who loves to be first,
will have nothing to do with us. So if I come, I will call
attention to what he is doing, gossiping maliciously about us.
Not satisfied with that, he refuses to welcome the brothers.
He also stops those who want to do so and
puts them out of the church.
—3 John 9-10

When the Yankees go out for dinner, they
reserve twenty-five tables for one.
—Author Paul Dickson

> When I was a little boy, I wanted to be a
> baseball player and join a circus.
> With the Yankees I've accomplished both.
> —New York sportswriter Murray Chass

The 2006 Yankees boasted one of the most formidable lineups ever, at least on paper. All nine of their starting players were all-stars. In the outfield they had Johnny Damon, Melky Cabrera, Gary Sheffield, Bernie Williams, and Hideki Matsui. As if that wasn't enough, they acquired Bobby Abreau from the Phillies at midseason. Around the infield they featured more stars, such as Jason Giambi, Derek Jeter, and quite possibly the best player in all of baseball, Alex Rodriguez. They also had super-rookie Robinson Cano at second base and veteran slugger Jorge Posada behind the plate. And many of their second-string players would have been starters on other teams.

But they weren't just dominating at the plate. Their pitching staff was one of the best in all of baseball. Imagine a quartet of Randy Johnson, Mike Mussina, Jaret Wright, and Chien Ming-Wang followed up by bullpen ace Mariano "Sandman" Rivera.

To be sure, an all-star lineup like this cost owner George Steinbrenner some serious coin. The payroll was reported to be at $200 million. But it seemed to be money well spent as the Yankees swept through the regular season, finishing 11½ games ahead of rival Boston. Sportswriters from around the country were already handing the Yankees their twenty-seventh World Series trophy.

But as the Yankees prepared to face the Detroit Tigers in the playoffs, there was rumbling from the clubhouse. One of the reasons the Yankees had so many stars on their roster was that several of their key players had been injured during the course of the season. As a result, the team went on the "rent-a-player" circuit at midseason and picked up stars from other teams. But then, as their own injured players began to get healthy and get off the disabled list, problems arose. Everyone wanted to start and be the star, but still there's room for only three outfielders at a time on the field. Add to that the perceived arrogance of certain players, and it was obvious that the clubhouse wasn't big enough for all of them.

In contrast to the Yankees, the Tigers were seen by the media as having no chance to win. Their payroll was less than half of what the Yankees' was, and they were a ragtag collection of aging veterans and young, wide-eyed rookies who had little postseason experience. Although they had played well for most of the regular season, they swooned late in the summer and didn't even win their own division.

But the Tigers seemed to have one advantage over the Yankees. They were a team on which each player put the other players first. And even though they weren't expected to win, they defeated the Yankees handily three games to one. The concept of team once again trumped the idea of individuality.

In the New Testament there is one mention of a church leader, Diotrephes. Little is known about him other than the fact that the apostle John said that he loved to be first, was a gossip, and refused to accept people into the church. The Greek word behind "loves to be first" here means "loves to be the leader." Diotrephes wanted to be in charge. He wanted to start, be the team leader, set the pace for everyone else. And he made sure that anyone else who wanted to come onto the team was given no place.

Diotrephes also accused others with his words. He gossiped about the apostle John and others. Gossip is a particularly hurtful use of words whereby one person tears down another. When we gossip, it's in an effort to show others that we are better. It's a form of comparison whereby we tell a story about someone, inferring "Of course, *I* would never do that."

Diotrephes also did his best to keep other Christians in the church from having a relationship with anyone who might threaten his authority.

Whether he did this by intimidation or by casting self-righteous shame upon the body of believers in his church, the end result was the same: he wanted to silence all his detractors so that he could remain on top.

But true leaders of God's team act quite differently. They don't lord it over others; instead, they set a Christlike example for them (1 Peter 5:3). Secure in Christ, they don't worry about the achievements or victories of another. They are more interested in building the kingdom of God than their own kingdom.

The 2006 Yankees had it all together on paper, but not in the clubhouse. Maybe they should have looked at their logo. Not only is there no "I" in team, there's no "I" in "Yankee" either.

intentional walk: Examine your own heart for a spirit of Diotrephes. Are you so competitive that it ruins your witness for Christ? Do you make room for someone else to lead or win, or do you do everything you can to make sure that you stay on top?

the faithful friend

A friend loves at all times,
and a brother is born for adversity.
—Proverbs 17:17

A man of many companions
may come to ruin,
but there is a friend who sticks
closer than a brother.
—Proverbs 18:24

[Bobby Doerr] is one of the few who played the
game hard and retired with no enemies.
—Tommy Henrich, Yankees outfielder

Bobby Doerr approached baseball the way he approached life: determined, consistent, no excuses, hard work, prayer, and faithfulness.

"I used to pray that I could be a major league ballplayer someday, and I thank God every night that he made this come true," recalls the oldest living member of the Baseball Hall of Fame. "Several things came up through my life that required that I have great faith in God and his Word in order to get through them."[1]

Doerr was a nine-time all-star second baseman with the Boston Red Sox from 1937 to 1951, and he was a slugger in an era when few middle infielders exhibited power. He drove in over one hundred runs six times, turned countless double plays with shortstop Johnny Pesky, and once held the American League record for handling 414 chances without an error. He was regarded by teammate Ted Williams as the silent captain of the Red Sox, and by everyone else as the nicest teammate a player could ever have. Bobby made a great impact on the Red Sox on the field, but his off-the-field contributions may have been even greater.

His teammate Ted Williams was known for his combative personality and for never losing an argument. Loud, profane, and defiant, Williams could make life miserable for those around him. By contrast, Doerr was quiet and sensitive, mature, and had an even-keeled spirit, compared to Ted's grandiose mood swings. But the brash Williams quickly realized that he needed a friend like Bobby, who could stay calm when Ted was exploding. And Bobby stayed faithful to Ted all his life.

There were times when even Ted Williams, the greatest hitter who ever lived, went through slumps, and Doerr could see what Williams was doing wrong at the plate. Anyone else who tried to correct Ted quickly got an earful from the proud hitter. But Bobby could gently make a suggestion to his friend and teammate, who accepted it and acted upon it. Ted had known Bobby since their first days in the minor leagues, so he trusted him. And in turn, Bobby stayed loyal to Ted, and at times he served as a buffer between him and the rest of the team and members of the media.

"Ted used to say to me, 'You read the Bible a lot, don't you?'" remembered Doerr. "And if you were around Ted much, you would never think he would end up in heaven. But knowing Ted Williams, he had about three different personalities. He was very stubborn, but he had a soft spot on the inside. Ted was known for not tipping his cap to the fans after hitting a home run, and was once asked in an interview about it. Ted responded to the reporter by saying, 'Many times I *did* tip my cap—on the inside.'"

But at the very end of his life, the brash Williams was thinking more humbly. "One night, toward the end of his life in the hospital," said

Bobby, "Ted sat up in bed and asked 'Do you think God would have me?' Of course, the answer would be yes for anyone who would admit their sins and confess Jesus as Lord. And I often wonder how many times Ted might have asked God on the inside for help, and I pray that he did before he died."[2]

It was while playing in the minor leagues that Bobby met his wife-to-be, Monica. She was a perky, redheaded schoolteacher who had been raised in the church, and she demonstrated a life of faith in front of Bobby every day. They were married for only nine years when she contracted multiple sclerosis. Not much was known about the disease in the 1940s, and although it was scary, her symptoms seemed to come and go.

But by the late 1960s, the disease was starting to affect Monica again, particularly her ability to walk. She went from a cane to a walker to a wheelchair, but Bobby never let it slow them down. When they traveled, he made special arrangements for her comfort. He stayed loyal to her, even in the days when she had nothing to give back but her spirit. By contrast, Ted Williams was married three times, and he infuriated a lot of other women who tried to get to know him.

In the 1960s the movie *King of Kings* was released, and Bobby watched it. "That movie really had an impact on me," he said. "The scenes and the music moved me to pick up the Bible and read the story of Jesus for myself. When I did, I began to learn and grow—and came to accept Christ as my Savior. There's life beyond baseball!"[3]

And knowing this was a real comfort to Bobby when Monica passed away after a third stroke in 2003. The couple had been married for sixty-five years. When the disease first came upon her, Bobby could have chosen to leave her. He was a famous baseball player with chiseled good looks and wealth, and surely he had other options.

But Bobby took his vows seriously. Monica lived with multiple sclerosis fifty-six years, and that means that Bobby lived with it for that long too. When the strokes began to come upon her, Monica had to be fed and bathed. Again, it would have been simpler to turn over complete care of her to someone else so that Bobby could have more time to fish and enjoy his retirement years. But he would have none of that. Bobby took care of Monica's physical needs until the day she died.

"Prayer was the secret to our long marriage," says Bobby. "It made us both stronger through the difficulties, and I will always be thankful for spending sixty-five years of my life with Monica. Being a baseball player was great, but my marriage was a much greater experience."[4]

God loves us with faithfulness and consistency that are unparalleled. There are times when we arrogantly try to live life our own way, but God gently comes to us and corrects our faults, and if we listen and obey his teaching, we find ourselves gaining new heights, free to stop repeating the same old mistakes. There are also times when we are disfigured and disabled with the disease of sin, and we might even wonder why God sticks around to gently take care of us and continue to meet our needs. But God does so because he is the Friend who sticks closer than a brother or sister. God is the one who loves us at all times and stands by us through adversity.

intentional walk: Faithful Friend, I thank you for sticking closer to me than anyone else on this earth. Your consistent devotion and loyal friendship woo me back to your side time and time again. I recognize that there are others who are not as fortunate as I am, and they need a faithful friend too. Lord, help me to befriend those who are unlovely, who have rough edges, and who cannot give me back anything in return. In doing so, may I be a living picture of Jesus to them—a model of determined love and faithfulness that sticks beside them even in the difficult times.

unfair comparisons

We do not dare to classify or compare ourselves
with some who commend themselves.
When they measure themselves by themselves and
compare themselves with themselves, they are not wise.
—2 Corinthians 10:12

When they operated, I told them to put in a Koufax fastball.
They did—but it was Mrs. Koufax's.
—pitcher Tommy John, recalling his 1974 arm surgery

Trying to hit him was like trying
to drink coffee with a fork.
—Pirates slugger Willie Stargell on trying to bat against Sandy Koufax

Sandy Koufax is the greatest Jewish athlete since Samson.
—George Jessel, America's "Toastmaster General"

Don Kessinger was a six-time all-star shortstop with the Chicago Cubs in the 1960s and 1970s before he closed out his career with the Cardinals and the White Sox. Although he was not a shortstop in the mold of today's power-hitting infielders, his RBIs were in his glove because the heart of the Cubs defense up the middle knew how to flash the leather. But in the summer of 1965, in his first full season in the majors, he was part of a game that went down in major league history.

The Cubs were in Los Angeles to face the Dodgers on September 9, 1965, and Kessinger humorously recalls the evening. "They had this old, broken-down lefthander named Sandy Koufax. He said he had a bad arm, and it was toward the end of his career. Early in the game, first inning, when a great pitcher's pitching, a guy comes in after hitting, and you always want to ask him, 'How's he throwing?' because you hope he'll say of the pitcher, 'He doesn't have anything tonight.'"[1]

Koufax, whose nickname was simply "The Man with the Golden Arm," is considered one of the greatest left-handed pitchers of all time, but at that point he hadn't won a game in three weeks. Plagued by arthritis in his elbow, Koufax pitched in constant pain for several years, and eventually he retired early, at the age of thirty-one.

The visiting Cubs batted first, and rookie Glen Beckert served notice that the Cubs were not going to back down, rifling a line drive down the left-field line that was foul by inches before he struck out. "Glen was my keystone mate at second base," recalls Kessinger. Beck came in and we said, 'How's he throwing, Beck?' and he said, 'He doesn't have it tonight, we're going to beat him.'"[2]

But if Koufax looked less than stellar in the first inning that night, the Dodgers must have thought that Cubs pitcher Bob Hendley was really Hall of Famer Bob Feller in disguise. Hendley allowed only one hit and one walk through the course of the game, but the Dodgers were able to eke out an unearned run for a 1–0 lead.

Perhaps one reason the Cubs had cause to be optimistic while battling against Koufax was the knowledge that Sandy was telegraphing his pitches. It was known around the league that a particular hitch in his windup could tell the batter whether a fastball or a curveball was coming. Yet even armed with that knowledge, the Cubs still struggled. Lamented future Hall of Famer Billy Williams, "We knew what was coming, and we still couldn't hit it."[3]

Hendley savors the moment, over forty years later. "That last inning, I remember people were standing on the dugout steps," Hendley recalled. "[Koufax] was coming out from under his hat after every pitch. You watch this guy, and you know this is special….But I've said it many times: If you're going to get beat, get beat by class. [Koufax] was the best."[4]

Kessinger recalls the night very well. "Well, Sandy is in Cooperstown for a number of reasons, and one of them is because that night he pitched a perfect game. Fourteen strikeouts. Twenty-seven up and twenty-seven down. And in the last two innings he struck out all six guys. Of course, we told Beck after the game, 'If he doesn't have it tonight, I'm not playing next time!'"[5]

Hendley was good—just not good enough. And Kessinger was reminded of a spiritual truth that night. "A guy like Sandy Koufax, every time he went to the mound, his intention was to pitch a perfect game. And that's the way the Lord would have us live our lives. He tells us in Matthew 5:48 to 'Be perfect, therefore, as your Heavenly Father is perfect.' Therefore the way we can get the most out of our Christian walk is not to compare ourselves to each other, like I'm better than this guy or that guy, but to compare ourselves to Christ, knowing that none of us can achieve perfection. Of course, he is faithful and just to forgive us when we fall short."[6]

It's easy to coast through life, comparing ourselves to one another. And it's amazing what passes for good until the real thing comes along. Hendley and Koufax came up about the same time, and both of them had careers that ended early due to arm injury. The similarities stop there, however. Hendley's won-loss record in the big leagues was decent at 48–52, but when Koufax retired, his record was 165–87, and he had cemented his reputation as one of the greatest left-handers in all of baseball history.

On my own, I might think I'm doing pretty well spiritually. I may not be better than the next person, but I'm no worse. And so it's easy to drift into spiritual complacency, comparing myself to others.

But try comparing yourself to Jesus. He is the standard by which our life will be measured. All of a sudden, words such as *decent*, *okay*, and *pretty good* don't apply to Jesus. Instead, words such as *holy*, *spotless*, and *pure* describe him, the only one who was worthy to pay the price for our sins. Maybe that's why more people don't go to church, read their Bible, or pray. They're afraid that if they get compared to Jesus, they'll see the real truth about their life.

intentional walk: You are "Holy, Holy, Holy," my Lord and Savior. My words fall far short of describing your perfection, and my life falls even further short of your holiness and glory. I thank you today, Jesus, for coming to earth to live a blameless life, to give me a model by which to live. And I thank you that even though I make mistakes every day, your grace is sufficient enough to cover all of my sins and cleanse me from all my unrighteousness. Help me to continue to compare myself to you every day, and at the end of this day, may I be a little more like you than I was at the beginning.

swinging

To keep me from becoming conceited because of these surpassingly great revelations, there was given me a thorn in my flesh, a messenger of Satan, to torment me. Three times I pleaded with the Lord to take it away from me. But he said to me, "My grace is sufficient for you, for my power is made perfect in weakness." Therefore I will boast all the more gladly about my weaknesses, so that Christ's power may rest on me.

—2 Corinthians 12:7-9

Anybody with ability can play in the big leagues. To last as long as I did with the skills I had, with the

> numbers I produced, was a triumph of the human spirit.…
> Instead of having the word "Powerized" on my bats,
> they say, "For Display Only".…I signed with the
> Milwaukee Braves for $3,000. That bothered my dad
> at the time because he didn't have that kind of dough
> to pay out. But eventually he scraped it up.
> —Bob Uecker, baseball comedian and a lifetime .200 hitter

In Little League, he swung at pitch after pitch, slowly learning how to make solid contact with the ball. As he grew, he kept swinging in Pony League, learning how to distinguish between a fastball and a curveball. And as he attended Redondo Union High School, he swung more and more. He was a star on the basketball team, but he enjoyed the mental challenges of baseball, and he kept coming back to the batting cage to take more swings.

When he graduated from high school, he enrolled at USC and made the baseball team as a walk-on. He kept swinging, kept practicing, and kept honing his skills at the plate and on the field. Major league drafts came and went each year he was in college, and the young man's name wasn't on anyone's list. So he kept swinging.

Finally, in 1998, USC's powerhouse baseball team won the College World Series, led in part by the Southern California native who enjoyed surfing as much as swinging the bat. He had a great year, batting .344 and leading the team with twenty-one home runs. After the national championship, USC's roster was raided by major league teams looking for fresh talent, and in the ninth round, the Houston Astros picked Morgan Ensberg, the kid who had been swinging a bat since the age of five.

Morgan rose through the minor leagues, developing a reputation as a strong hitter who was also a decent fielder. By 2003 he was installed as the everyday third baseman on an Astros team that usually was in contention each year to make the playoffs. And Morgan kept swinging, hitting .291 with twenty-five home runs in his first full season.

In 2005 the surfer-turned-swinger had a career year, bashing 36 homers, 101 RBIs, and finishing fourth in the National League MVP voting. He was a major part of the Astros team that went to the World Series that year.

And then his swing stopped connecting.

Morgan's batting tailed off after the 2005 season. Plagued by injuries, he found out how quickly the media and fans could turn on someone who was putting up less-than-stellar numbers. He swung through pain, through stints on the disabled list, and through demotions to the minors, but he couldn't recover his stroke. He was traded toward the end of the 2007 season to the Padres, where he kept swinging, but his average and power continued to plummet. In 2008 he was picked up by the Yankees, swinging all the way, but his numbers hovered around the dreaded Mendoza Line. In midseason he was let go, and he signed a minor league contract with the Indians.

But through it all, Morgan Ensberg kept on swinging—not for the reason you might expect. "I don't look at baseball as anything different than what other people do," says the man who once was on the NL all-star team. "God always places us in spots where he needs work done."[1]

Ensberg remembers a special epiphany that he had a few years ago. "In 2005, when the Astros were going to the World Series, I was taking batting practice in the cage one day, and all of a sudden it hit me that I'd been taking thousands and thousands of swings, playing baseball since the age of five. Everyone knows your goal when you're playing baseball is to make it to the big leagues. That's the whole purpose of all the practice.

"But that day in the batting cage, it dawned on me that the real purpose for all that practice I had done in my life through Little League, high school, and college and the minor leagues wasn't to get to the big leagues. Instead, it was so I could show people that Jesus Christ is my Savior. For others, they may think they are working hard for their job's sake—for their company or whatever—but it just clicked that the only reason I was taking extra hitting practice was for God's purposes. It was an awesome moment, to realize that God had a plan for me that started back when I was five, and really before that!"[2]

A more cynical person might think that Morgan would do well to concentrate more on his hitting so that he could stay in the majors. But this man goes out day after day, trying to do his best. He's not motivated by individual awards and achievements. He's motivated only to know and do God's will for his life. "We all think we're working for our job, but the reality is that God puts his purpose on our lives," says the man who would like to take seminary classes after his career is over. "Sure, I feel closer to him when everything's going really well. But my performance in baseball and my faith in Jesus Christ have nothing to do with each other. I realize that God has an ultimate plan for me, and whether or not I'm doing well or poorly is not going to make me question God's will."[3]

One might think that Morgan would be different hitting .220 instead of .320. But the little boy in the veteran third baseman shows up every day with the same exuberance, the big grin, the kind eyes, and, of course, his swing. His joy isn't dependent upon his performance.

"I want to conduct myself in a manner that is pleasing to God, whether I'm doing well or poorly," he says. "Baseball is my job, but Jesus

Christ is my life. And it's too easy to think that when good things happen in my life that it means that God is with me, and when bad things happen, it means he's not. See, I believe that God can use us even when we're struggling. In fact, he may use us in an even greater way when we are struggling."[4]

The apostle Paul certainly found that to be true. When you talk about someone who had struggles, you can't leave this biblical hall-of-famer off the list. Through prison, floggings, stonings, shipwrecks, bandits, hunger, thirst, and untold dangers and pressures, he kept his eyes on Christ and fulfilled God's purpose for his life. We mostly recall his triumphs, tending to forget that his life was an epicenter for spiritual warfare as he evangelized and poured out his love for churches with his letters to them, which eventually became accepted as Scripture. Paul wanted to be released from whatever weakness plagued him, but he found that his weaknesses forced him to depend on God even more; and that was a good thing, because his own strength wasn't going to get the job done. Only when he was weak could God's strength be displayed in him.

"Those situations in Houston were very difficult," admits Morgan. "And it goes against so much in me, but sometimes I pray, 'God, put me in uncomfortable situations,' because it forces me to lean on Christ. I can't do it myself. Put me in tough spots, because it's in the tough spots that I learn that I need you. So I pray that God would put me in places where he would allow others to come to know Christ through me."[5]

So Morgan prays hard in whatever city he's playing for at the time. But he does more than pray. He swings.

intentional walk: Lord, I admit that I keep trying to give you my strengths, to serve you without any hint of weakness for fear that people will see me at less than my best. Take my weaknesses, and if you have to put them on display so that others can see how strong you are compared to me, then so be it. Through my failures and difficulties, help me to keep swinging and never give up, knowing that your purposes for my life are really the only things that matter.

outside the box

So God created man in his own image,
in the image of God he created him;
male and female he created them. God blessed
them and said to them,
"Be fruitful and increase in number; fill the
earth and subdue it. Rule over the fish of the sea
and the birds of the air and over every living
creature that moves on the ground."
—Genesis 1:27-28

The only way I'm going to win a
Gold Glove is with a can of spray paint.
— Hall-of-Famer Reggie Jackson

> They should've called a welder.
> —Phillies announcer Richie Ashburn, watching notoriously
> poor fielder Dave Kingman's glove being mended during a game

Do you consider yourself to be a creative person? Most people relegate creativity to artists or musicians and don't think of themselves as very imaginative or innovative. But to be created in God's image means that we have the capacity to know him and, in some sense, to become a small picture of what he is like. Since God is a creator, there is a part of us that glorifies him when we use our creative ability.

God set us on this earth with this simple command: fill the earth and subdue it. Of course, we can't create out of nothing, as God did when he created the heavens and the earth. But we can take the raw materials that God has created and subdue them or otherwise reshape them and put them to use to serve others. Bill Doak might not have said it that way, but that's exactly what he did.

Bill Doak's name isn't found in Cooperstown, at least not directly. He was a very good pitcher in the 1910s and 1920s who won 169 games for the Cardinals and led the National League in ERA twice. His thirty-two shutouts are second in Cardinals history to the great Bob Gibson. He was also considered a "straight arrow," the only strictly moral man on the Cardinals. He had a fine career, but his numbers are shy of the Hall of Fame.

Few people have heard of Bill Doak. But young boys all across the country in the 1920s–1950s knew his name, even if they knew next to nothing about his career. In fact, his name came up every time Christmas or a boy's birthday came around. Kids wore his name on their hand every time they played the game in a sandlot or a back alley. This was because Bill Doak was a creative fellow and a man who loved God and served him as a Sunday school teacher. And it's also because Bill Doak invented the baseball glove as we know it today.

The first gloves used in the game were just that—gloves. Sometimes the fingers were torn away to allow for a better grip on the ball. The fingers weren't connected or laced together. Occasionally, a pad was inserted in the palm to take away a bit of the sting. But a baseball glove around 1900 was thought of as a protective device, not as a tool to help a fielder catch the ball. If you have some sort of glove you wear in the winter, take a look at it, and know that the men in your family one hundred years ago would have played baseball with it.

Equipment in baseball evolved slowly, and much of it was invented not by some creative scientist in a laboratory but rather by the very men who played the game and realized out of necessity that there had to be a better way. They thought outside the box, were first ridiculed over their inventions, and then praised. An example is Roger Bresnahan, a catcher from a century ago, who helped create or further develop most of the gear that catchers wear today. He was taunted by other players, but it's not hard to imagine why he invented shin guards. What's hard to understand is why it took fifty years or so for someone to come up with them.

Bill Doak came up with the Reds in 1912, but he stuck for good in the big leagues with the Cardinals the next year. He was a spindly player who struggled with back problems and didn't have an overpowering fastball. But he rode the spitball (legal in the era in which he played) to great success, pitching two complete game victories in one day in 1917 and winning twenty games in 1920.

His greatest achievement, however, came off the field in the front offices of the Rawlings Sporting Goods Company. Bill suggested a new design for a baseball glove, complete with webbing laced between the thumb and forefinger, something that gloves had never had before. He explained, "By enlarging the thumb, bringing it up even with the first finger, a larger pocket is formed and many balls are caught on the very tips of the thumb and first finger."[1]

A pocket in the glove made it possible for fielders to catch and trap the ball safely with one hand and take away much of the sting. It also increased the range of fielders, who now could reach for a ball to the side and not have to be directly in front of it to catch it. Almost overnight, Bill Doak model gloves were being worn by players at all levels of competition. The sales of the glove actually netted Bill more income than his baseball salary, as Rawlings produced the basic Bill Doak model glove from 1920 through 1953.

Although it wasn't as important as, say, a cure for a disease, Bill's invention did change the face of the game of baseball. And in his modest, unassuming way, Bill simply saw himself as simply fulfilling God's command on his life to subdue the earth, to create because he was made in the image of his Creator.

Maybe we fail to think outside the box because it requires faith, and it's always easier to walk by sight than by faith. To be creative, we must sometimes refuse to do things exactly the way they were done in the past, and for most of us, it's easier to go with what we believe is the "tried and true" formula instead of asking God to show us a better way. But those who ask God to give them creative answers to problems find great victory in walking by faith.

It was an outside-the-box solution to battle when Gideon dismissed thousands of his soldiers and pared his force down to only three hundred (Judges 7). It certainly wasn't reasonable for David to shun Saul's armor in favor of a sling and five smooth stones (1 Samuel 17). And it wasn't logical for Moses to lead the children of Israel across the Red Sea (Exodus 14).

But when the people of God follow him by faith, they find a better way to live. Their problems don't go away, but they find that God brings all his creative resources to bear on their situation and gives them innovative solutions as they trust him.

intentional walk: Are you facing a sticky problem that requires outside-the-box thinking? Do you feel like you're stuck in a rut while others produce in clever, imaginative ways? You don't lack creativity. What you lack is faith to believe that God has your answer. Seek God today and ask him to spark the gifts that he has given you, that you might be an original for him. After all, there's no one else he created exactly like you.

home

Hence! Home, you idle creatures, get you home!
—Flavius, in *Julius Caesar*, by William Shakespeare

In football the object is for the quarterback, also known as the field general, to be on target with his aerial assault, riddling the defense by hitting his receivers with deadly accuracy in spite of the blitz, even if he has to use the shotgun. With short bullet passes and long bombs, he marches his troops into enemy territory, balancing this aerial assault with a sustained ground attack that punches holes in the forward wall of the enemy's defensive line. In baseball the object is to go home!
—Comedian George Carlin

But in keeping with his promise we are looking forward to a new heaven and a new earth, the home of righteousness.
—2 Peter 3:13

the double win

Do nothing out of selfish ambition or vain conceit, but in humility
consider others better than yourselves. Each of you should look not
only to your own interests, but also to the interests of others.
—Philippians 2:3-4

I always turn to the sports section first. The sports section records
people's accomplishments; the front page nothing but man's failures.
—Earl Warren, Chief Justice of the United States, 1953–1969

Everyone dreams about hitting a home run to win a game. Even the late
inning sub whose pants are full of splinters fantasizes of coming off the
bench to launch one over the fence and win the game for the team. This
is true whether you are a guy or a gal.

In late April of 2008, with the season winding down, two northwestern women's softball teams were battling in a tournament to see who would go on to represent the conference in the NCAA (Division II) regional playoffs. The Wolves of Western Oregon were visiting the Wildcats of Central Washington University in Ellensberg, playing a doubleheader. Neither team had ever represented the Great Northwest Athletic Conference (GNAC) in postseason play.

Central Washington was led by their slugging first baseman, Mallory Holtman. Holtman was the career home run leader in the GNAC and eventually was named as the conference player of the year for women's softball. Western Oregon was in first place, led by a host of strong players. But because there was a doubleheader scheduled for the day, both teams had to utilize some of their bench players.

Sara Tucholsky was a senior outfielder for Western Oregon who had been used sparingly during the season and had struggled to find her swing. Coming into the doubleheader, she was batting .138. She had played as a late-inning substitute in the first game, in which the Wolves had crushed the Wildcats 8–1, but she started the second game in right field. The young woman just 5 feet 2 inches tall, had never hit a home run in either high school or college, and she realized that with limited playing time, her dreams of clearing the fence might never happen.

But sometimes dreams do come true.

With no score in the top of the second inning, Tucholsky came to bat with two runners on base, and on a 0–1 count put every ounce of her petite frame into a pitch that she drove over the centerfield wall. The fans in attendance cheered, and her teammates came off the bench in celebration. Excited as she began to run the bases, Sara rounded first, and the two runners ahead of her scored. That's when it all went wrong. Sara missed first base.

It happens. In the excitement, running through new territory, feet can slip, legs can misstep. Sara realized her mistake and spun around to return to touch first base. When she did, something popped in her right knee, and she fell to the ground. Writhing in pain, she slowly crawled back and clung to the bag as time was called. Umpire Jacob McChesney wondered to himself, "What on earth are we gonna do?"[1]

Western Oregon coach Pam Knox wisely recognized that if players from the Wolves touched Sara, she would be declared out. No teammate can provide assistance to another teammate as they run the bases. Yet if Sara didn't finish her journey on the base paths, her home run would count only as a single. Instead of a 3–0 lead, the score would be 2–0. Moreover, Sara's dream of hitting a home run would be wiped out of the box score.

It was at that point that help arrived from an unlikely source. Mallory Holtman, of the Central Washington team, had an idea. "I approached the umpire and asked, 'What if *we* pick her up and carry her?'" she explained after the game. "He looked at me kind of strange, but he said 'Yes, you can do that.'"[2] So, despite the fact that it would cause their team to be down by one more run, Holtman and teammate Liz Wallace picked Tucholsky up and began to carry her around the bases.

All three girls were laughing by the time they got to second base, wondering what it must look like to the fans in the stands. "The only thing I remember is that Mallory asked me which leg was the one that hurt," Tucholsky said. "I told her it was my right leg and she said, 'OK, we're going to drop you down gently and you need to touch it with your left leg,' and I said 'OK, thank you very much.' She said, 'You deserve it, you hit it over the fence,' and we all kind of just laughed."[3]

When Holtman and Wallace touched Sara's foot to home plate, they surrendered her to her teammates and returned to their positions, still determined to compete against the team that they had just helped, still determined to win the game even though they were now down by three runs. They pushed two across the plate in the bottom half of the inning, but it wasn't enough, and Western Oregon went on to sweep the doubleheader and advance to the NCAA regional tournament. The girls from Central Washington had lost.

Or had they?

"In that situation, you don't really think about the wins and losses, you just think 'This person is in pain, and she needs help,'" said Holtman in an interview. "She hit it over the fence….Anyone's deserving of a home run when they hit it over the fence….My main concern was her and the quicker we could get her in to see a trainer, because she was in agony, so it was the right thing to do."[4]

There's an old axiom: "If I win, I win for me, but if I help you win, I'm a double winner."

The box score would show only seventy-five in attendance that day. The official press release simply read, "Tucholsky homered to center field, 3 RBI." The scoreboard display was "Visitors 4, Home 2." But none of these reflected the real winners. Holtman and Wallace had stopped to consider what was truly important, and in doing so, they became winners too.

As followers of Christ, we are called to put others first and to help make other people winners. But it's so easy to get caught up in the things of this world and to seek only our own gain. Jesus could have done that. He could have decided that equality with God was something to be grasped, a brass ring to be seized at the expense of all humanity. Instead, he chose differently, paying far too high a price for the likes of the human race. In doing so, he made us winners, more than conquerors really (Romans 8:37), and experienced the glory of being a double winner.

intentional walk: Jesus, I'm so used to pursuing my own goals that I'm often insensitive to the needs of others around me. Slow me down today, Lord, and when the opportunity arises to meet someone else's needs, even at my own expense, remind me that I'm simply serving you with all my heart.

help from the bench

Therefore, since we have a great high priest who has
gone through the heavens, Jesus the Son of God, let us hold
firmly to the faith we profess. For we do not have a high
priest who is unable to sympathize with our weaknesses,
but we have one who has been tempted in every way,
just as we are—yet was without sin. Let us then approach
the throne of grace with confidence, so that we may
receive mercy and find grace to help us
in our time of need.
—Hebrews 4:14-16

That isn't an arm, that's a rifle.
—Catcher Gene Tenace, seeing Johnny Bench throw to second base

I don't want to embarrass any other catcher by
comparing him with Johnny Bench.
—Sparky Anderson, Reds manager

If you're a man, you probably don't like to ask for assistance when you
need help. The old line "When men are lost, they don't ask directions,
they just buy another tank of gas" says it all. Actually, both men and
women are slow at times to admit not knowing something, and we'd
rather just keep going the same direction and hope that we figure it out
somewhere along the way. But that doesn't work in the big leagues. Just
ask Eddie Taubensee.

Taubensee was a rarity: a catcher who bats left-handed and had some
pop in his bat. He played for ten years, mostly with Cincinnati, and had
a great year at the plate in 1999, batting .311 with 21 homers and 87
RBI. Eddie definitely knew his way around the plate when he had a bat
in his hands, but not so much when he had to strap on a mask and chest
protector and get behind the plate.

"As a young catcher with the Reds, I was known as primarily an
offensive catcher, but I got labeled as being not very good defensively,"
he remembers. "It's tough to shake those labels. It's true—I had a
tough time holding the running game in place, and I struggled to throw

out runners at second base. I was platooning with veterans like Benito Santiago and Joe Oliver, fighting for playing time, and I sure didn't feel I could ask them for help. I couldn't tell the pitchers I was struggling, because they don't want to hear that you can't throw anybody out at second base, and I sure didn't want to tell the coaches, because if I told them, I would lose playing time. I felt all alone, and didn't think anyone could help me. But ultimately, if you play a lot, you can't hide your struggles," says the now-retired player, who works for Pro Athletes Outreach, a ministry to professional athletes and their families.

"One of our coaches, Ray Knight, knew I was having trouble, and he said, 'Why don't you come to the park early tomorrow morning, and we'll work on your throwing.'

"I was eager to put in extra work and improve my game. But I didn't feel a whole lot better when he added, 'And Johnny Bench will be there to help you.'

"See, Johnny Bench is considered the greatest catcher of all time, and he has this aura around him in Cincinnati. Now, he didn't come into the locker room very often. Maybe at spring training or the beginning of the year, but not in midseason. I was thinking, *Oh boy, I must be doing bad, they had to drag Johnny Bench off the golf course to help this young struggling kid.*

"I was very intimidated. I showed up the next day, but instead of going out onto the field, we worked in a cage underneath the stadium. It almost felt like a secret mission—here's the catcher of all catchers taking time for me.

"As Johnny was talking to me about my mechanics—what to do with my feet, what to think about while I was catching, he pointed me back in the right direction. It didn't take him long, only an hour or so. He knew exactly what I was going through. After all, he was a Hall of Fame catcher. He had put the gear on himself, he had been in those pressure-filled situations trying to hold a runner on first base, and he knew how to get me through it.

"I was like a kid in a candy store—I hung on to every word that came out of the lips of Johnny Bench. When I put those things he taught me into practice, I began to see some results, and my defensive game improved,"[1] concluded Taubensee, reflecting on his eleven-year big league career.

Jesus, the King of all kings, came down and strapped on human flesh. He experienced everything that we go through—joys and sorrows, exhaustion and hunger, elation and disappointment. He shared in our humanity, and he knows what it's like when we are tempted to sin, because he was tempted in every way too. The difference is that he never once sinned.

He became what we are so that he might make us what he is.

And since faith comes by hearing the Word of God (Romans 10:17), we need to be willing to receive instruction from him and hang on his words. But we don't have to be intimidated to ask him for help. In fact, we can walk right into his locker room, and even though he wears an aura of holiness about him, we can boldly ask him for help and direction for our lives. He's not a grizzled veteran who ignores us, fearful that we'll take his job. Instead, he's the Ancient of Days, who already knows what's on our hearts before we voice our requests.

intentional walk: Lord, sometimes I am intimidated to come into your presence. Your light shines so brightly, and there is often so much darkness in my life. Help me to remember that, as your child, I always have a place at your table, and that you are always willing to help me as I fumble through this life. May I find solace and strength when tempted, knowing that you can identify with my pain. And may I always look to you for the way out when I am tempted (1 Corinthians 10:13).

silence isn't golden

At the end of seven days the word of the
LORD came to me: "Son of man, I have made
you a watchman for the house of Israel; so hear the
word I speak and give them warning from me.
When I say to a wicked man, 'You will surely die,'
and you do not warn him or speak out to dissuade
him from his evil ways in order to save his life,
that wicked man will die for his sin, and I will
hold you accountable for his blood. But if you do
warn the wicked man and he does not turn from his
wickedness or from his evil ways, he will die for
his sin; but you will have saved yourself."
—Ezekiel 3:16-19

You know…the only thing we have left in this world is
our judge and the twelve jurors and they found me not guilty.
They do some funny things in baseball."
—Buck Weaver, shortstop, 1920 Chicago White Sox

Run an Internet search for the name "Buck Weaver," and you'll see that in 1920 George Daniel "Buck" Weaver hit .331 at the age of thirty, his final year in baseball. If it seems odd that someone would leave baseball voluntarily in the prime of his career, it should. The happy-go-lucky infielder with the irrepressible smile seemed primed for several more years of stardom.

Then again, Buck Weaver didn't leave baseball on his own terms.

Weaver played nine seasons with the Chicago White Sox, and he gained a reputation as a competitive shortstop and third baseman who "guarded the spiked sand around third base like his life." It was said that even the fleet-footed Ty Cobb wouldn't bunt when Weaver played third, knowing that he could be thrown out. Weaver, also known as the "Ginger Kid," steadily improved with the bat as he learned to switch hit, and he hit over .300 in the 1917 World Series.

The White Sox looked to be a dominant force in the American League during the 1910s–1920s. Enjoying the fruits of a new stadium, Comiskey

Park, they featured star players such as Weaver, pitcher Eddie Cicotte, future Hall of Famers Ray Schalk, Red Faber, and Eddie Collins, and legendary hitting machine "Shoeless" Joe Jackson.

But while White Sox owner Charles Comiskey was known to spend lavishly on his ballpark and the fans, he was tightfisted in his dealings with the players. Not only did he underpay most of his team, but also, in an attempt to reduce the team's laundry bills, he often forced them to play in dirty uniforms. As a result, the press took to calling the team the "Black Sox."

Toward the end of their successful 1919 season, eight different White Sox players met with gamblers before the World Series, and seven agreed to lose several of the games in exchange for cash. The lone holdout was Buck Weaver, who refused to participate. During the series, while several of his teammates were dropping fly balls, swinging at bad pitches, and running slowly on the base paths, Weaver was hitting .324 and fielding flawlessly at third base. Unfortunately, it was not enough, as the White Sox threw the World Series to the Cincinnati Reds.

When the story became public at the end of the 1920 season, the players were put on trial and were found innocent in a court of law. But newly appointed baseball commissioner Kennesaw Mountain Landis banned all eight players for life, stating that "no player that sits in conference with a bunch of crooked players and gamblers where the ways and means of throwing games are discussed and does not promptly tell his club about it will ever play professional baseball."[1]

Devastated by the decision, Weaver spent the rest of his life trying to clear his name. It was obvious that he had played well in the 1919 World Series. And he never accepted any money to throw the games. But if silence is a crime, Buck Weaver was guilty. He had known the truth about the fix, but he had done nothing to stop it and hadn't told anyone about it.

As a follower of Christ, you know that the "fix is on" in this life. Our sworn enemy has come to "steal and kill and destroy" everything about our lives (John 10:10). We can bury our heads in the sand, ignoring what is at stake, and convince ourselves that all is well with us. But may heaven spare us from thinking that because all is well with us, all is well with the rest of the world.

You are called to be a "watchman" on the wall, a sentry posted on guard at the gate, and to alert others to approaching danger. The best way you can do that is not to memorize some sort of prayer formula that you can get others to recite. Nor is it to become sort of a zealot, pounding your Bible into the face of strangers on the subway or at work.

No, the best way you can alert people to the approaching danger is simply to love them with the love of God and, at the appropriate time, share your story of how God has changed your life. God holds us accountable for those we could have loved but didn't. God gives us the responsibility of speaking up to tell the truth, to share the gospel. As the brother of Jesus said in James 4:17, "Anyone, then, who knows the good he ought to do and doesn't do it, sins." And when we share the love of God with others, our lives are flooded with joy.

Embittered by his ordeal, Weaver wrote letter after letter to the commissioner of baseball, arguing his innocence. In an interview shortly before his death, the man who used to play ball without a care in the world stated, "A murderer even serves his sentence and is let out, [but] I got life."[2] Unfortunately for Buck, he lost the joy of his youth as he spent the rest of his days trying to clear his name. He found out too late that silence isn't golden.

intentional walk: O God, forgive me for the times I have kept the truth of your love to myself. I know the good that I should do and the people around me who need a witness. But there is a disconnect between my knowledge and my actions. May your kingdom come, Lord, and your will be done in my life down here. Help me to simply love them as Jesus would, and as I do so, may it please you to bring some of them into a right relationship with you.

a blood-bought victory

Then Jesus went with his disciples
to a place called Gethsemane, and he said to them,
"Sit here while I go over there and pray."
He took Peter and the two sons of Zebedee along
with him, and he began to be sorrowful and troubled.
Then he said to them, "My soul is overwhelmed
with sorrow to the point of death.
Stay here and keep watch with me." Going a
little farther, he fell with his face to the ground
and prayed, "My Father, if it is possible, may
this cup be taken from me. Yet not as I
will, but as you will."
—Matthew 26:36-39

A minute that used to recur like a comet, once every 86 years
or so and missed by generations of Red Sox fans,
is now beginning to feel like a birthright.
—Gordon Edes, *Boston Globe* writer on the second
Red Sox World Series victory this century

Curt Schilling's road to major league stardom has had a lot of twists and turns in it. He spent a few years with the Orioles and the Astros before finding success on the mound with the Phillies, then becoming a great postseason pitcher with the Diamondbacks and the Red Sox. Along the way, his wife battled cancer, and despite the Walter Mitty lifestyle of a big league player, Schilling was tired of waking up every morning without real purpose in his life.

That began to change when he realized his need for a Savior in 1997. Driving home one day, he began to pray the first of many prayers that he would pray in his life, praying the Lord's Prayer and slowly beginning to understand that Jesus was the Son of God and the Savior, not only of Curt, but also of the world.

And Curt kept praying, though he didn't make a big deal about his newfound faith. But slowly and deliberately, things began to change in his life. He found that his addiction to tobacco began to fade away.

Though he remained intensely competitive, he found that he didn't want to hate anyone anymore. He began to realize purpose and meaning for his life, and slowly he began to build his faith in Christ into the foundation of his family.

But his faith really grew during the 2004 postseason, especially as he learned what *not* to pray for. Schilling suffered a torn tendon sheath in his right ankle during the division series against the Angels, and gamely he tried to pitch on it in the first game of the American League Championship Series against the Yankees. The Bronx Bombers exploded for six runs off Schilling and went on to win the game. Afterward, doctors performed an experimental procedure on the ankle to try to enable him to pitch another game in the playoffs, and so they created a crisis of faith for the big right-hander. Because Curt wanted to win, but knew that he had to resign his will to that of his heavenly Father.

With the guidance of his pastor before the sixth game, Schilling began to pray, but he didn't pray that he and his team might win the game. Instead, he prayed for the strength to compete, believing that God would give him strength to do his best. He also resolved to give God the glory after the game, whatever the outcome.

The Yankees faced a man on a mission that night, a man who had discovered that God's purpose for his life was more than just personal success on the mound. With blood seeping through his sock, Schilling pitched masterfully through the pain, allowing only one run, and the Red Sox went on to beat the Yankees for the right to play in the World Series against the Cardinals.

At the press conference after the game, Schilling said to reporters, "Seven years ago I became a Christian, and tonight God did something amazing for me. I tried to be as tough as I could, and do it my way Game 1, and I think we all saw how that turned out. Tonight it was all God. I knew that I wasn't going to be able to do this alone. And I prayed as hard as I could. I didn't pray to get a win or to make great pitches. I just prayed for the strength to go out there tonight and compete, and he gave me that. I can't explain to you what a feeling it was to be out there and to feel what I felt."[1]

Schilling was slated to start the second game of the World Series, but on the morning of the game he woke up and was unable to walk. Doctors attended to the sutures in his ankle, hoping for the best. And Curt was resolved that he would not deter from God's game plan for his life at this critical juncture. He once again prayed before the game, understanding that prayer was not a way of telling God what to do but rather a way of submitting his will to God's.

"And then I did what I did the last time: I went to the Lord for help, because I knew, again, I wasn't going to be able to do this myself,"[2] he said later. And the results? Same story, second verse, and with historical results. The Red Sox won the game and eventually swept the Cardinals in the World Series—the first time the team had won a championship since 1918, when Babe Ruth was the star of the team.

Curt Schilling's experiences illustrate the need for the right kind of praying in our lives. He was probably tempted to ask God for a win in those situations, to pray for his own success and glory. James cautions us against such praying when he says, "When you ask, you do not receive, because you ask with wrong motives, that you may spend what you get on your pleasures" (James 4:3).

But two thousand years before Schilling's bloody sock and a World Series victory, there was another who shed his blood and brought us victory on an infinitely greater level. Jesus showed that he was completely committed to God's plan for his life when he prayed, "Yet not as I will, but as you will." And even though that plan involved a cross, Jesus submitted to his Father, determined that God get the glory for whatever would happen.

And God did. And God still does every time a follower of Christ prays the right kind of prayer.

intentional walk: Father, we both know that I'm a bag of mixed motives as I pray. Please forgive me for the times I've tried to use you for my own personal gain. You're not the Santa Claus of the sky; you are the Holy Lord of the universe. If your Son was required to submit to your will, how much more I must be committed to know and do your will for my life. May the words of my Savior "Yet not as I will, but as you will" be the ending of all my prayers and the overriding desire of all my heart.

vapor trail

Now listen, you who say, "Today or tomorrow we will go to this or that city, spend a year there, carry on business and make money." Why, you do not even know what will happen tomorrow. What is your life? You are a mist that appears for a little while and then vanishes. Instead, you ought to say, "If it is the Lord's will, we will live and do this or that." As it is, you boast and brag. All such boasting is evil.

—James 4:13-16

There is one word in America that says it all, and that one word is, "You never know."

—Joaquin Andujar, Cardinals pitcher

Ten feet tall and bulletproof—that's how we typically see our baseball heroes. They can run faster, throw harder, and hit farther than any of us, so their bodies shouldn't be susceptible to the same ailments, diseases, and accidents that we encounter, right?

Except life just doesn't work that way. Bad and good stuff happens—to everyone. The rain falls on both the righteous and the unrighteous, according to Jesus (Matthew 5:45). Even the Lord had to go through trials in his body and spirit, so why would we think that any of our modern-day heroes are any different?

Tony Conigliaro is a great example of "What if?" "Tony C" was highly regarded in Boston when he first came up with the Red Sox. A native of the back alleys of Boston, he hit a home run off the first pitch he ever saw at Fenway Park. In his second season he led the league in home runs. He became the youngest player, at the age of twenty-two, to reach one hundred career home runs.

But at the age of twenty-three he was cut down by a fastball that broke his left cheekbone and caused severe damage to the retina of his left eye. He attempted to come back a couple different times, but he was never the same player. At the age of thirty-seven he had a heart attack, then a stroke, and existed in a coma for the last eight years of his life.

Lou Gehrig's name may be more synonymous with the terrible disease that was named after him, but before he contracted amyotrophic lateral sclerosis, he was the "Iron Horse," the beloved, slugging first baseman for the Yankees who played in 2,130 consecutive games before the disease began to ravage his body. He passed away at the age of thirty-eight.

And then there's the sad story of Don Wilson. The Houston Astros right-hander had a fastball with a vapor trail and could heat up the air-conditioned Astrodome with his "cheese at the knees." In his rookie season he threw a no-hitter. The next year, he tied the then major league record by striking out eighteen batters in one game. The following year, he threw another no-hitter. Along the way, he also made the all-star team and, in a controversial move in another game, was pulled after eight innings despite the fact that he was still pitching a no-hitter!

But Don Wilson didn't just throw fast; he lived fast. Constant late-night partying and an abrasive personality kept him in trouble with the management and also kept him from realizing his full potential.

"He would often sit beside Ken Forsch and myself in the locker room before games," recalls Tom Griffin, another flame-throwing pitcher with the Astros during those days. "He'd say, 'I notice the way you guys show up for work—you're consistently ready to play, and you seem to have something different about you.' Ken and I would share thoughts about Christ with him. Don would respond by saying that he already believed in God, but he wasn't ready to make a commitment to Christ as Lord of his life."

During the winter after the 1974 season, Wilson, Griffin, and some others had been assigned to lead a pitching clinic at an area high school and play an exhibition game. "We did the clinic, but Wilson never showed up," says Griffin. "The next morning I got a call from the Astros general manager that Wilson and his son had died in some sort of accident."[1]

It was later revealed that Wilson had been drinking, and the previous night, he pulled his car into his garage and shut the garage door automatically. But he never turned the car engine off, and he passed out behind the wheel. The garage was attached to the house, and not only did he die from the carbon monoxide in the car's exhaust, but also his young son, sleeping upstairs in the house, died in his sleep, and his wife and daughter were hospitalized.

Griffin tenderly remembers the funeral. "I was a pallbearer and was there when the casket closed. Here was a guy who knew he needed to make a commitment to Christ, but no one can know for certain if he ever did. Don was always counting on tomorrow, but this time tomorrow never came."

Wilson's death was senseless but not without lasting impact. "Because of the tragedy of Don Wilson, I can say that I am more bold in sharing my testimony. I serve in my local church with a large group of sixth-graders, and I find myself wanting to share God's love with them more and more," says Griffin.[2]

When we're young, we view ourselves as invincible, indomitable. "Bad stuff" happens to other people, not us. But Scripture clearly teaches that we are here today and gone tomorrow. There are no guarantees. Our life is just a mist, a vapor trail, much like the all-too-brief fastballs that Tony Conigliaro hit, or Lou Gehrig caught, or Don Wilson threw.

intentional walk: What if you had only twenty-four hours to live? Would you live any differently? How would it change your priorities? And what if you lived every day of your life as if it were your last? Psalm 90:12 says, "Teach us to number our days aright, that we may gain a heart of wisdom."

last at bat

For the kingdom of heaven is like a landowner who went out early in the morning to hire men to work in his vineyard. He agreed to pay them a denarius for the day and sent them into his vineyard. About the third hour he went out and saw others standing in the marketplace doing nothing. He told them, "You also go and work in my vineyard, and I will pay you whatever is right." So they went. He went out again about the sixth hour and the ninth hour and did the same thing. About the eleventh hour he went out and found still others standing around....

He said to them, "You also go and work in my vineyard." When evening came, the owner of the vineyard said to his foreman, "Call the workers and pay them

their wages, beginning with the last ones hired
and going on to the first."

The workers who were hired about the
eleventh hour came and each received a denarius.
So when those came who were hired first, they
expected to receive more. But each one of them
also received a denarius. When they received it, they
began to grumble against the landowner.
"These men who were hired last worked only one hour,"
they said, "and you have made them equal to us who
have borne the burden of the work and the heat of the day."

But he answered one of them, "Friend, I am not
being unfair to you. Didn't you agree to work for a denarius?
Take your pay and go. I want to give the man who was
hired last the same as I gave you. Don't I have the right to
do what I want with my own money?
Or are you envious because I am generous?"
So the last will be first, and the first will be last.

—Matthew 20:1-16

[Ty] Cobb lived off the field as though he wished to live forever.
He lived on the field as though it was his last day.
—Branch Rickey, Brooklyn Dodgers manager

Heaven will be filled with surprises. Chief among those may be the realization of who is and who isn't there. There will be some people whom we expect to see because they appeared to be so spiritual, so good here on earth. But some of these will be the ones of whom Jesus says, "Go away from me. I never knew you" (Matthew 7:23). There will be others who will take our breath away as we see them for the first time in heaven. "You? You are a follower of Christ? I never would have guessed."

But whether one arrives at the vineyard early and puts in a full day's work or arrives at the end of the day and works only for an hour, all are paid the same wages by the Master. Such will be the case of Ty Cobb.

Tyrus Raymond Cobb was a polarizing figure, and most people who knew him quickly decided that they wanted to be poles apart from him. His drive to succeed at any cost was most likely the result of his domineering and perfectionist father, who caused Ty to carry the burden of great expectations all his life. No matter how hard he tried, Ty's efforts were never good enough to please his father.

But at the age of seventeen, unthinkable tragedy struck. Ty's father suspected his mother of carrying on an adulterous affair, and on one out-of-town trip, he deliberately returned early to the Cobb home, thinking that he would catch his wife being unfaithful. She was alone, but thinking that Ty's father was a burglar, she shot the intruder in the middle of the night, mortally wounding him. In the crazy way that young adolescents get things mixed-up, Ty absorbed a ton of guilt for what happened to his father, believing that somehow it was his own fault. He bore the pain of that tragedy the rest of his life, displaying a passion fueled by anger every time he came to bat or ran the base paths.

Most baseball players try to keep their emotions in check, realizing that when they get angry on the field, they lose their composure and their game as well. Not Ty. He vented his rage on coaches, umpires, other players, and, of course, the baseball itself. Cobb's lifetime records are the stuff of legend: a .367 lifetime batting average, 892 stolen bases (including 35 thefts of home), 4,191 hits, and 12 batting titles, including 9 in a row. He batted over .400 three times and under .320 only once.

Yet despite his success on the field, Ty had few friends. Early in his career he was subjected to the usual hazing that all rookies endure. Instead of good-naturedly enduring the ribbing and teasing, Ty sullenly withdrew from his teammates, speaking to them only when he was angry. He demanded perfection from others, which didn't win him any fans in the clubhouse. Infielders who played against Cobb as he ran the base paths often ended the game with their uniforms shredded by Ty's sharp spikes, which he was reputed to sharpen before games.

Off the field, Cobb also struggled. He went through women like he went through his whiskey: hard, fast, and continuously. He was known to be a racist, an adulterer, a profane man, and according to his own testimony, he once beat a man within an inch of his life in a brawl, leaving him unconscious and not breathing.

Yet Cobb was also moved by the plight of the less fortunate in society. Once his ball playing days were over, he invested money in a little-known Georgia business, the Coca-Cola Bottling Company. The growth of his stock through the years allowed him to contribute funds to the widows of former ballplayers (this was before major-league baseball had a pension fund of any kind). He also started a college scholarship program for needy Georgia students, and he donated money to start a hospital in Royston, Georgia, which eventually grew into the Ty Cobb Healthcare System, which even today serves rural areas in Georgia.

Despite his efforts to even the scales of right and wrong in his life, Ty never could have done enough to earn his way into heaven. And so it was at the very end of his life that the man known as the "Georgia Peach" had his greatest hit.

His body riddled by cancer and wracked by chronic pain, Cobb spent the last year of his life in and out of hospitals and doctors' offices. One physician in particular, William Nesbitt, was a young Christian doctor, and he attempted to minister to Ty spiritually as well as physically: "Over the years, whenever I'd visit, Cobb would ask me to read the Bible and pray with him. I recognized his spiritual hunger, evident in his attentiveness to God's Word. I felt that God had given me a unique opportunity to share. Some of Cobb's requested passages were Psalm 91 and Isaiah 53. The words of 1 Corinthians 13, 'And though I bestow all my goods to feed the poor, and though I give my body to be burned, and have not love, it profiteth me nothing,' seemed to convict him."[1]

In May of 1961 Ty was admitted to the hospital for the last time and was visited by a local pastor, John Richardson. The pastor simply read Scripture and prayed with him on the first quick visit. Days later the pastor returned, and he found Ty to be more open to talk about spiritual things. "I explained God's plan of salvation and the need for repentance," recalled Richardson. "He replied that he wished to put his complete trust in Christ. On subsequent visits Ty was eager to talk about Jesus Christ. Two days before his death, I paid my last call. 'I feel the strong arms of God underneath me,' Ty said. 'It is wonderful to be able to pray. Tell folks they should not wait as I did, until a crisis comes, before they learn how.'"[2]

Some will say that there's no room for Ty in heaven, that his blatantly sinful life should keep him out. But if that's true, then God will have to throw out a lot of other people—all of them, in fact. It's true that no one can know for sure about another person's relationship with Christ, but Romans 10:9-10 says that we must simply confess that Jesus is Lord with our mouth and believe with our heart that God raised him from the dead. And judging from the testimonies of Nesbitt and Richardson, we can believe that Ty did that.

No, he didn't start working in the vineyard early in the day. In fact, he barely made it to the vineyard before the workday was finished. But he did make it. And the generous Master rewarded him with the same reward that he gives those who have followed Christ all their lives.

It's called grace. No, Ty didn't deserve it. But neither did Billy Graham, Mother Teresa, or even the apostle Paul. Neither do you or I.

So, in the ball game of your life, what inning are you playing in right now? Truthfully, none of us know. You can put off a relationship with Christ, saying, "I'll take care of that God-relationship thirty minutes before I die." That would not be an acceptable answer even if you knew when that would be. But baseball is a funny game. No one really knows what time the game will end. It might even be called off early.

If Ty could say one thing to us today, he might say, "Don't wait for the ninth inning. Place your trust in Jesus now, while you can still serve him during the game of life. It's never too late."

intentional walk: Dear God, it's hard to imagine that you would still love me and want me after all I've done. But your Word says over and over that you do. And if grace is still available for my life, then I want it and need it. I confess that you are Lord, Jesus, and that you rose from the dead. Please come into my life and forgive me of all my sins—past, present, and even future. And help me, so that I might have an intentional walk with you all the days of my life.

notes

introduction

1. From "High Flight," by John Gillespie Magee Jr. (http://www.skygod.com/quotes/highlight.html)

first

The Little Things

1. Dianne Baker, "Sharing a Love for the Game," in *The Softball Coaching Bible*, ed. Jacquie Joseph (Champaign, IL: Human Kinetics, 2002), 6.

There *Is* Crying in Baseball

1. George W. Nicholson, "Kindred Spirits, Humble Heroes: Branch Rickey and William Wilberforce" (http://www.humanevents.com/article.php?id=19979).

2. Ibid.

Your Ticket Is Punched

1. 714—the number of home runs Babe Ruth hit; 1927—the 1927 Yankees are often considered the greatest team in history; 61—number of home runs Yankee Roger Maris hit in 1961, eclipsing Babe Ruth's record of 60; 26—the Yankees have won 26 world championships. No other team has won even half as many.

Babe on Babe

1. "Babe Pinelli" (http://en.wikipedia.org/wiki/Babe_Pinelli).

2. Babe Pinelli, "God, Family, Country, and Baseball" (http://www.thisibelieve.org/dsp_ShowEssay.php?uid=16890).

The Fading Glory of Kings

1. Attributed to Andy Warhol, quoted in *Washington Post*, November 15, 1979 (http://www.bartleby.com/63/19/5419.html).

Death of a Dream

1. Jim Morris, "Jim Morris on 'The Rookie,'" video clip on Reel Faces (http://www.chasingthefrog.com/reelfaces/therookie.php).

2. Jim Morris, "The Rookie," on Reel Faces (http://www.chasingthefrog.com/reelfaces/therookie.php).

second
Hear Here
1. Harry J. Heintz, "Hearing with the Heart," *Leadership* 15, no. 2 (http://www.preachingtoday.com/illustrations/weekly/98-07-01/3653.html).

2. Bill Nichols, "Pride Conquers Hearing Defect," *Cleveland Plain Dealer*, June 17, 1993 (http://www.lkwdpl.org/nworth/pride.htm).

No Shortcuts
1. Al Worthington, interview by Hugh Poland, May 28, 2008.

Lefty's Blaze
1. Paul Dickson, *Baseball's Greatest Quotations: An Illustrated Treasury of Baseball Quotations and Historical Lore*, rev. ed. (New York: Collins, 2008), 224.

2. "Lefty Grove, Hall of Fame Pitcher, Dies," Associated Press, May 23, 1975 (http://www.thedeadballera.com/Obits/Grove.Lefty.Obit.html).

3. Frank Pastore, interview by Hugh Poland, October 11, 2006.

4. Andy Stanley, "Dealing with Anger" (http://www.preachingtoday.com/sermons/sermons/265.html).

Eyes on the Prize
1. John Thorn, "Rube Waddell: The Peter Pan of Baseball" (http://www.mrbaseball.com/index.php?option=com_content&task=view&id=21&Itemid=57).

The Pitch That Changed Everything
1. Frank Pastore, interview by Hugh Poland, October 11, 2006.
2. Ibid.

third
Crossing the Line
1. Paul Dickson, *Baseball's Greatest Quotations: An Illustrated Treasury of Baseball Quotations and Historical Lore*, rev. ed. (New York: Collins, 2008), 165.

2. Willie Aikens, interview by Hugh Poland, via letter postmarked February 7, 2007.

The Natural
1. Evan Grant, "Faith Brings Texas Rangers' Hamilton Back from the Brink," *Dallas Morning News*, February 29, 2008.

2. Grant, "Faith Brings Texas Rangers' Hamilton Back from the Brink."

3. Albert Chen, "The Super Natural," *Sports Illustrated*, June 2, 2008, 35.

4. Keown, "I'm Proof That Hope Is Never Lost."

The Faithful Friend
1. Bobby Doerr, interview by Hugh Poland, August 4, 2006.

2. Ibid.

3. James D. Smith III, "Bobby Doerr in 1934: His Reflections on Life in Pacific Coast League at 16," *The National Pastime*, January 1, 2005, 88.

4. Bobby Doerr, interview by Hugh Poland, August 4, 2006.

Unfair Comparisons
1. Don Kessinger, interview by Hugh Poland, August 12, 2006.

2. Ibid.

3. "Sandy Koufax's Perfect Game" (http://en.wikipedia.org/wiki/Sandy_Koufax's_perfect_game).

4. Phillip Ramati, "Former Pitcher Bob Hendley Recalls His Date with Fame,"

Baseball Digest, December 2005 (http://findarticles.com/p/articles/mi_m0FCI/is_ 10_ 64/ai_n15784092/pg_3?tag=artBody;col1).

5. Don Kessinger, interview by Hugh Poland, August 12, 2006.

6. Ibid.

Swinging

1. Morgan Ensberg, interview by Hugh Poland, May 13, 2008.

2. Ibid.

3. Ibid.

4. Ibid.

5. Ibid.

Outside the Box

1. Steve Steinberg, "Bill Doak," *Deadball Stars of the National League* (Cleveland: Society for American Baseball Research), 358.

home

The Double Win

1. "Touching Them All," ESPN video (http://sports.espn.go.com/broadband/video/ videopage?videoId=3380875).

2. Ibid.

3. "Sara Tucholsky," *Chicago Tribune*, May 1, 2008 (http://www.chicagotribune. com/sports/chi-sara-tucholsky-080501-ht,0,2783629.story).

4. Interview of Mallory Holtman, "ESPN First Take" (http://www.youtube.com/ watch?v=Bbqv14oFOf4&feature=related.)

Help from the Bench

1. Eddie Taubensee, "2006 Home Plate with the Paints!" audio sermon delivered July 16, 2006, at Calvary Baptist Church, Chillicothe, Ohio (http://www.sermonaudio.com/ search. asp?SpeakerOnly=true&currSection=sermonsspeaker&keyword=Eddie%5Etaubensee).

Silence Isn't Golden

1. David J. Fletcher, "Buck Weaver," *Deadball Stars of the National League* (Cleveland: Society for American Baseball Research), 513.

2. Ibid.

A Blood-Bought Victory

1. Drew Zahn, "Baseball Pitcher Schilling Sustained by God," *Preaching Today* (http://www.preachingtoday.com/illustrations/weekly/04-11-01/15601.html).

2. Jackie MacMullan, "Painful Day, Then Win Sewn Up," *Boston Globe*, October 25, 2004 (http://www.boston.com/sports/baseball/redsox/articles/2004/10/25/painful_ day_then_win_sewn_up?pg=full).

Vapor Trail

1. Tom Griffin, interview by Hugh Poland, December 14, 2004.

2. Ibid.

Last At Bat

1. William R. Nesbitt Jr., "What Ty Cobb Really Wanted," *Today's Christian*, May/June 2001 (http://www.christianitytoday.com/tc/2001/003/6.37.html).

2. John R. Richardson, "Don't Wait as Long as I Did," *Today's Christian*, May/June 2001 (http://www.christianitytoday.com/tc/2001/003/7.41.html).

select name
and subject index

SELECT NAME AND SUBJECT INDEX

scripture index

ALSO BY HUGH POLAND

Steal Away: Devotions for Baseball Fans

"Through a vast knowledge of America's greatest pastime, Poland weaves together a winning combination of great baseball quotes with various impacting passages of Scripture." —CBN.com, The Christian Broadcasting Network

"Thoughtful and thought-provoking, *Steal Away* is very highly recommended reading for all Christian baseball fans." —*Midwest Book Review*

"I sense in *Steal Away* a familiar passion both for baseball and for following Christ." —from the foreword by Mariano Rivera, New York Yankees
978-0-8170-1491-9 $13.00

The Master Carpenter: Devotions for Woodworkers

"Every library and woodshop should have this book! Keep *The Master Carpenter* close at hand for daily reflection and inspiration as you seek to apprentice yourself to Jesus." —from the foreword by Scott Phillips, woodworker of *The American Woodshop* (PBS)

"Hugh Poland does an exceptional job of connecting faith and life in Christ to every aspect of woodworking....Woodworkers will appreciate Hugh's creative and thought-provoking approach." —from the preface by Bob Hunter, tools & techniques editor, *WOOD Magazine*

"Tons of scriptural references and quotes, along with Poland's insights, recharge a woodworker's spiritual batteries with a power even greater than lithium-ion." —Joanna Takes, senior editor, *Woodworker Journal*
978-0-8170-1529-9 $15.00

Books are available at Christian bookstores nationwide or from Judson Press at www.judsonpress.com.